holy
and acceptable

building a pure temple

David Edwards

LifeWay
LifeWay Christian Resources
Nashville, Tennessee

Produced by:
National Student Ministry Department
LifeWay Christian Resources
127 Ninth Avenue North
Nashville, Tennessee 37234
Customer Service: (800) 458-2772

Editor: Art Herron
Production Specialist: Leanne B. Adams
Graphic Designer: Bob Redden

Dewey Decimal Classification: 613
Subject Heading: HEALTH SELF-CARE \ CHRISTIAN LIFE

Scripture quotations marked NIV are from the Holy Bible, *New International Version,* copyright © 1973, 1978, 1984 by International Bible Society. Used by permission.

Scripture marked NASB is taken from the *NEW AMERICAN STANDARD BIBLE,* © Copyright The Lockman Foundation, 1960, 1962, 1963, 1968, 1971, 1972, 1973, 1975, 1977, 1995. Used by permission.

ISBN 0-7673-9428-3

contents

holy and acceptable
building a pure temple

about the writer

about the writer

David Edwards speaks from his heart about issues relevant to generation X. He has been featured speaker for City Wide Weekly Bible Study Groups in Texas, Oklahoma, Alabama, Arkansas, Mississippi, Louisiana, Georgia, and Florida. Recently he was on seventeen college campuses with CrossSeekers events.

David graduated from Oklahoma City University with a BA in Religious Education and has completed work toward a Masters from Southwestern Baptist Theological Seminary, Ft. Worth, Texas. David's mission is to reintroduce the truth of God's Word by meeting people where they are in life and bringing them one step closer to knowing and becoming like Jesus Christ.

Dave is author of the book *One Step Closer,* creator and speaker for the *Destination: Principles for Making Life's Journey Count* four-part video series, and author of the witnessing booklet "how to make life all good." He also writes for *Christian Single* and *Living Solo* magazines.

david edwards

Thanks to:

Trey Bowden, who taught me that what is mightier than the pen and the sword, is the keyboard.

The mighty Flingers for parenting me in purity. Ms. Fingerly, your life still inspires me.

The CrossSeekers® Covenant

"You will seek me and find me when you seek me with all your heart." Jeremiah 29:13

As a seeker of the cross of Christ, I am called to break away from trite, nonchalant, laissez-faire Christian living. I accept the challenge to divine daring, to consecrated recklessness for Christ, to devout adventure in the face of ridiculing contemporaries. Created in the image of God and committed to excellence as a disciple of Jesus Christ,

INTEGRITY

I will be a person of integrity

"Do your best to present yourself to God as one approved, a workman who does not need to be ashamed and who correctly handles the word of truth." 2 Timothy 2:15

My attitudes and actions reveal my commitment to live the kind of life Christ modeled for me—to speak the truth in love, to stand firm in my convictions, to be honest and trustworthy.

SPIRITUAL GROWTH

I will pursue consistent spiritual growth

"So then, just as you received Christ Jesus as Lord, continue to live in him, rooted and built up in him, strengthened in the faith as you were taught, and overflowing with thankfulness." Colossians 2:6-7

The Christian life is a continuing journey, and I am committed to a consistent, personal relationship with Jesus Christ, to faithful study of His Word, and to regular corporate spiritual growth through the ministry of the New Testament church.

WITNESS

I will speak and live a relevant, authentic, and consistent witness

"Always be prepared to give an answer to everyone who asks you to give the reason for the hope that you have." 1 Peter 3:15

I will tell others the story of how Jesus changed my life, and I will seek to live a radically changed life each day. I will share the good news of Jesus Christ with courage and boldness.

SERVICE

I will seek opportunities to serve in Christ's name

"The Spirit of the Lord is on me, because he has anointed me to preach good news to the poor. He has sent me to proclaim freedom for the prisoners and recovery of sight for the blind, to release the oppressed, to proclaim the year of the Lord's favor." Luke 4:18-19

I believe that God desires to draw all people into a loving, redeeming relationship with Him. As His disciple, I will give myself to be His hands to reach others in ministry and missions.

PURITY

I will honor my body as the temple of God, dedicated to a lifestyle of purity

"Do you not know that your body is a temple of the Holy Spirit, who is in you, whom you have received from God? You are not your own; you were bought at a price. Therefore honor God with your body." 1 Corinthians 6:19-20

Following the example of Christ, I will keep my body healthy and strong, avoiding temptations and destructive personal vices. I will honor the gift of life by keeping myself sexually pure and free from addictive drugs.

CHRISTLIKE RELATIONSHIPS

I will be godly in all things, Christlike in all relationships

"Therefore, as God's chosen people, holy and dearly loved, clothe yourselves with compassion, kindness, humility, gentleness and patience. Bear with each other and forgive whatever grievances you may have against one another. Forgive as the Lord forgave you. And over all these virtues put on love, which binds them all together in perfect unity." Colossians 3:12-14

In every relationship and in every situation, I will seek to live as Christ would. I will work to heal brokenness, to value each person as a child of God, to avoid petty quarrels and harsh words, to let go of bitterness and resentment that hinder genuine Christian love.

Foreword

Sexual Purity:
A Lifelong Commitment

By Richard Ross

In 1993 a small group of high school students met to discuss how they could make a difference related to sexual purity among other high school students. Out of this meeting emerged a worldwide campaign designed to challenge teenagers to make a promise to God to abstain from sex until they enter a biblical marriage relationship. In 1994 over 211,000 signed True Love Waits commitment cards — enough to cover the National Mall in front of the nation's capitol. In 1996 over 350,000 commitment cards were stacked to the roof of the Georgia Dome in Atlanta.

It is now estimated by LifeWay Christian Resources that over a million teenagers have made a True Love Waits commitment. This figure is based on the number of commitment cards distributed through LifeWay and information from the National Longitudinal Study on Adolescent Health.

Less than 60 teenagers were in that first group. Wow! What an impact God has created from the hearts of teenagers seeking to do a godly thing with their bodies. God was faithful to use their commitment to begin a worldwide program of sexual purity. As you read this book, you may be one of the hundreds of thousands of college students who signed a commitment card years ago. It is my desire that you find ways to share this commitment with other collegians to begin a worldwide movement of sexual purity on your campus. Just because you entered college or graduated from high school, the commitment has not ended.

My guess is as a college student or a young adult, your commitment has been challenged as never before. Maybe it's because you are more adult now; maybe it's because you are seeing sexual temptation in different settings and your values are tested every day. The value of sexual purity until marriage is questioned on most college campuses.

I am grateful that National Student Ministry of LifeWay Christian Resources has provided you and thousands of other college students an excellent resource dealing with purity. *Holy and Acceptable* by Dave Edwards speaks to the core of the issue for you as a college student.The purity of your heart will determine most of the decisions you make on campus or as a young adult. Many times the decisions you face as a college student blurs a commitment made five or more years ago. You find yourself on a campus where it seems no one knows or cares about a spiritual commitment you made during high school.

The purity of your heart provides a clean heart God can use. What would happen if suddenly a call for sexual purity emerged from among the millions of college students? What if a small group on campus makes a covenant through CrossSeekers to remain a person of biblical purity? They can impact college campuses throughout the world.

As a college student, it is now your turn to make a difference on your campus. A campus, I might add, which is totally different from your high school campus and all the friends you had there to support the True Love Waits decision.

I highly recommend *Holy and Acceptable* to you if you've ever signed a True Love Waits commitment card. If you are just now joining the True Love Waits movement or desire to be sexually pure until marriage, *Holy and Acceptable* will provide lifestyle choices which are pleasing to God through a life dedicated to purity.

Let me encourage you to find or create a CrossSeekers Covenant Group on your campus. It may meet in your church or through a religious campus organization. Binding yourself in covenant with God and with other Christian students will bring life-changing experiences you will enjoy.

Many of you will meet your mate during the college years. Here's hoping that you will meet sexually and morally pure. That is my prayer for you and all students on your college campus.

A Simple Introduction

We live in a *postmodern** nation that offers a smorgasbord of beliefs promising to bring meaning and happiness to our lives—like believing new tennis shoes will get you an express ticket on the Hale-Bopp Comet to heaven to the idea that researching your family tree will get you your own planet. Our problem is that we have stacked so many beliefs on our plate, and now all the juices have run together.

When it comes to absurd ideas, our nation is better stocked than a Golden Corral buffet. I've never figured out why the pineapple and the gravy are next to each other. Ideas are like food; some of them just don't go together.

For too long, too many of us have gazed through the spit guards at the buffet of beliefs. We've sampled a little bite of Buddhism and a morsel of Mormonism. We've taken more samples than Puff Daddy. Our souls are a gooey mixture of mystic theology that goes together about as well as Carmen and Courtney Love. Something has to change.

It's time for some spring cleaning. You're growing up, and you need to get rid of some of the stuff you've outgrown—the jumbo jerseys, the L.A. sag, and wearing your hat backwards (unless you're a rapper or a catcher)...but I digress.

This *postmodern* world is textured with ideas about purity. We pick the ideas we like the best and the ones that fit what we are doing for the moment. We shop for beliefs like we shop for clothes. What we buy depends on where we're going and whom we'll be with. Purity isn't relative to where we are or whom we are with. If it changed with the people or the situation, we couldn't call it pure.

Our lives are complicated with beliefs that confuse us. We need to clear our soul's plate and ask one question: "What does God want?" Living in the will of God will make life uncomplicated. *And simple is better.*

It was Soren Kierkegaard, the famous philosopher dead guy who said, "Purity of heart is to will one thing." Our lives must be simplified and must be founded on one thing.

Jesus put it this way, *"I love the Father and that I do exactly what my Father has commanded me"* (John 14:31, NIV). Jesus' life flowed from the recognition of this simple truth. "The will of God is good." That belief shaped His emotions, actions, and words. He simplified life and lived it perfectly.

Purity is simple—it's one thing. Purity is seeking to do God's will in every situation you face.

"He who loves purity of heart and whose speech is gracious, the king is his friend" (Prov. 22:11, NASB).

The focus of this book is the CrossSeekers Covenant principle of purity, which states, **"I will honor my body as the temple of God, dedicated to a lifestyle of purity."** The word *covenant* is a big fancy Bible term for the will of God. This book is about establishing the will of God through the principle of purity in your life.

To be holy and acceptable in God's sight means you choose purity in a *postmodern* world. This book will help you find your way to a pure heart and to will one thing that will make your life all good. I've tried to make the study of this subject simple for those of you who have had too much NutraSweet in your diet.

Here's a simple outline to help you keep it simple:

Simple Beliefs Produce Supernatural Behavior
Start with Christ, who lives in you.
    Identify the seeds of self-destruction.
        Manage your thought life.
            Plan your personal convictions.
                Live by design.
                    Exchange wrong decisions for right ones.

Each of the six sessions in this book focuses on one of these six simple beliefs. As you study each of them, you will be challenged to apply them to your life. As you choose your beliefs about purity, I hope you choose purity of heart and seek the one thing that matters...***the will of God.***

—Dave Edwards

* *Postmodernism can be partially defined as a way of looking at life which declares that there are no absolutes, that truth is relative, that pluralism supercedes sectarianism, and that individualism rules over collectivism.*

a moment of clarity

Start with Christ, who lives in you.
Identify the seeds of self-destruction.
Manage your thought life.
Plan your personal convictions.
Live by design.
Exchange wrong decisions for right ones.

A Moment of Clarity

"He who loves purity of heart and whose speech is gracious, the king is his friend" (Prov. 22:11, NASB).

Lately there has been so much emphasis put on sexual purity that we have overlooked the rest of our lives. When it comes to integrity in relationships and conversations, we're not pegging the needle on the honesty meter. We say one thing and mean another.

He said. She said.

When she says, "Do you think she's pretty?" **she means,** "Deny it, or this will be one of the most unpleasant days of your life."
When she says, "Wherever you want to go is fine," **she means,** "Whatever you choose will be wrong."
When she says, "I don't want to talk about it," **she means,** "You'd better ask me what's wrong 50 more times!"

When he says, "I'm really busy," **what he means is,** "*Baywatch* is on."
When a guy says, "I could never date anyone else," **he really means,** "...because I'd get caught."
When a guy says, "It's a 'guy-thing,'" **he means** that there is no rational thought pattern connected with it whatsoever.

Here are some for you to translate.

When a girl says, "I don't have anything to wear," what she means is

When a girl says, "Does this make me look fat?" what she means is

When a guy says, "That was a really good movie," what he means is

When a guys says, "I love you," he really means

What are some of the polluted thoughts you have caught running through your mind?

What are some of the things or phrases you've caught yourself saying that shine a light on the pollution that's really inside you?

What are some of the choices you've made that let other people see what you really don't want them to see?

Surveys show that the main difference between believers and non-believers having sex is that after believers have sex, they pray for forgiveness.

We violate the ethic of purity in our thinking. The violation shows up in our conversations and ultimately in the actions we choose. Just like the "He said. She said." exercise above, we take the first step away from purity when what we say and what we mean don't match. *Purity is just a concept until we choose to make it a part of our thoughts and words.* Until purity is established in our thoughts and words, it will not affect the choices we make.

All of us face some struggle for purity. **There are those things within us that we will not violate, and yet we seem to be tested at these points on a regular basis.** Some of us have already given up on the notion that there is a standard for purity other than our own. Surveys show that believers have the same sexual desires as non-believers. *Surveys show that the main difference between believers and non-believers having sex is that after believers have sex, they pray for forgiveness.*

This book is to help you understand that God's view of purity involves every area of your life, not just what you do sexually. Our study of purity will lead you to examine the motives, intentions, and myths that determine our approach to purity.

We need to come to the place where our lives form a distinct difference the world can't help but see. The distinction has to be more than just a different lifestyle; it has to be a **meaningful lifestyle.** We have to know why we *think* and ultimately *choose* what we do.

Our struggle to establish purity springs from the myths we have chosen to believe. Maybe you'll find yourself in one or more of the following myths.

Myths about purity

"Purity is only about what I do sexually." God's Word tells us to be an example of believers in the things we say, the way we behave, our love, our faith, and our purity. Purity is about what you do sexually, but it starts long before the act of sex. It starts in the thoughts we think. See the truth in 1 Timothy 4:12.

"It's too late for me...I've made too many mistakes." Some people disregard purity, thinking that it's too late to deal with the issue of purity for their lives. God is the Father of second chances. It's never too late for purity. It's never too late to change the thoughts you think, the words you say, and the choices you make. The only deadline for purity is death. See the truth in Isaiah 1:18.

"I'm not religious enough." The *"religion myth"* seems to be a favorite among students today. They use it to rationalize their own misbehavior. "I'm not religious, because I'm wild." If you don't believe in purity, any excuse will do. Until you choose to value God's values more than you value your own values, you'll never value purity. See the truth in 2 Timothy 2:22.

"If I choose to do the purity thing, everything will be 'all good' all at once." The consequences for our choices are not going away. We all have to be mature enough to face the consequences of the choices we've made and learn from them to make the wise choices in the future. See the truth in Galatians 6:7.

"God will give me whatever I want, if I just stay pure." When I hear this, I hear students doing the "implied leverage thing," that is, "God owes me to make my life work, because I've made all these sacrifices for Him." See the truth in Hosea 6:6.

"I'm a Christian because of the things I don't do." Do we really think God measures our lives from the outside when the Bible clearly teaches that He looks on the heart? We are Christians only when Christ comes to live within us, and our choices for behavior should reflect the changes He has made and continues to make within us. I talk with students all the time who think they can refrain from having sex and still be pure, even though they purposely continue to think polluted thoughts and speak garbage. See the truth in 1 Samuel 16:7.

"Purity is God imposing His will on me." God is the perfect all-powerful gentleman. There is no door that He can't knock down. He could easily impose His will on us, but He has chosen to allow us to choose the paths for our lives. When I willfully choose God's standards for my life, I find the best and highest call that life has to offer. See the truth in Deuteronomy 30:19.

> Which of the myths listed above holds a position of power in your life, and why have you chosen to believe it?
> Use this space to write your response.

Purity begins with a choice to pray and ask God for the help to make purity permeate every area of your life. If you're ready, you can start with the prayer below.

"God, I really do want to take steps toward building Your purity into every area of my life. Please make me sensitive to the lies I sometimes believe about purity. Give me wisdom to take steps toward being free from these myths. Amen."

Something is going to form the foundation of your thoughts, words, and actions. You might as well build your foundation from the principles of God's Word.

I like to call this section **Purity 101.** It comes from Psalm 101. Thus, the 101.

King David is the author of this Psalm. He was called a man after God's own heart, because he had embraced the heart of the KING. He knew the only way his life would work would be if it were built on the principles of purity.

These are the three foundational principles that the ethic of purity is built on:

Principle One: **Purity forms powerful results.**
"I will sing of lovingkindness and justice..." (Ps. 101:1, NASB).

The benefits of God are more than theory—they are reality. David experienced the powerful benefits of God and he couldn't help but sing about them. His song comes out of the overflow of his pure heart before God. He sings his song so we can know that these powerful results are only produced and experienced when purity is anchored in our lives.

Intimacy with God. Simply put, godly purity brings you intimately close with God. The Bible is full of men and women who were surrounded by the blessings and miracles of God. They had their share of struggles, but through it all, they had the knowledge that God was watching out for them. *"Blessed are the pure in heart, for they will see God"* (Matt. 5:8, NIV).

You'll better interpret your emotions. Emotions can blind us and lead us to think that we are better off than we really are. Purity acts like a life preserver for our souls. Instead of just treading water in the storm, we are able to use the emotional energy to set sail in the right direction.

Thankfulness. God has a plan for you to experience the best life has to offer, and you can have that. When you begin to experience the best life has to offer, you'll be thankful.

Respect. Biblical purity eliminates many of the relationship games people play. Respect dictates that we see people as sons and daughters of God, not pieces of meat. The "He said. She said." communication game is replaced with genuine honesty. When this

What other benefits of building your life on purity can you think of?

Why is God's approach to purity better than your approach?

kind of purity runs throughout your life, people see the genuine way you treat others, and they give it back to you in abundance.

Clear Conscience. One of the most powerful results of purity is a clear conscience. Wouldn't it be great to live a life where the "No Fear" logo was tattooed on your heart? A clear conscience is attainable through practiced biblical purity.

> It's all about your focus. Your *yes* must be bigger than your *no.*

Principle Two: **Purity must flow out of a positive, passionate relationship with God.**

"Every morning I will destroy all the wicked of the land, so as to cut off from the city of the LORD all those who do iniquity" (Ps. 101:8, NASB).

Things I need to destroy every day of my life...

David was saying that each morning he would make a daily choice to establish purity in his life. His daily priority was to protect the dwelling place of the Lord. He gave God an ultimate yes for everything he did that day. The purity that flowed out of his passionate relationship with God was his most prized possession. It was his passion for God that gave him the energy to remain pure. If we try and live a pure life for any reason other than a positive, passionate relationship with God, we will burn out. Where is your focus?

Our focus should be on the One who loves us more than we can love ourselves. Anything our passion for Him leads us to give up or do without is nothing when compared with the surpassing value of knowing Him. It's not the *THINGS* we say *no* to, it's *WHO* we are saying *yes* to.

God,
"I love You so much that I want our relationship to be positive and passionate. I know that if I'm not extremely careful, other things can and will dilute our relationship. So I have taken the time to list some of the things that I need to destroy every day of my life. I'm asking You to help me grow our love so that I want You more than anything else. I also need Your help day by day to remove these things from my life until they are a memory and not a reality. I really do want to be more in love with You than I am with myself."

Principle Three: **Purity flourishes when practiced rigorously.**

"I will give heed to the blameless way....I will walk within my house in the integrity of my heart" (Ps. 101:2, NASB).

David saw himself as the home of God, and he had resolutely chosen to walk in purity. He was committed to making every area of his life a place where God could feel comfortably at home. The more he practiced it, the more purity filled his life, until he could say that integrity was the hallmark of his heart.

Not long ago, I met some friends for dinner. We joined up at a girl's house. We walked in, and her living room was more than tidy, it was immaculate. Not a speck of dust, the couch cushions were spot free, and the drapes looked like they had just gotten back from the cleaners. We had experienced a terrible thunderstorm a few days before, and this girl told us that during the storm her dog had gotten so scared that he attacked her bedskirt and tore it off. I wanted to see the damage, but she blocked the way to her room and begged me not to go in. I had to know what else she was hiding. I finally managed to get around her and open the door! Her clothes looked like they were crawling out of the drawers. The lamp was completely off the table, and the curtains were in shreds. Shoes hung from the mirror, her bed looked like it hadn't been made in a month, and she had a big brown trash bag full of garbage right in the middle of the room. She was worried about the bedskirt. I folded my arms, and with all the sincerity of an interior decorator, I told her, "I love what you've done with the place...the only thing missing is the chalk outline of a body."

We love to keep the living rooms of our lives clean and spotless, because most people never see the real mess in our private areas. If we would just put equal emphasis on all areas of our lives we could avoid these embarrassing moments. David tells us that he kept his life clean so that anyone walking by could look in and find no barriers to the beauty God was building in his life.

It's vital to make the practice of purity a daily priority. You never know who will walk into your life.

**Purity is expressing my love for
God in every area of my life.**

Practicing private purity precedes public performance.

The rest of Psalm 101 is a practical guide to help us identify some key areas to watch and to make sure we practice purity. This is not a comprehensive list, but it does cover the biggies. Once you faithfully work on these major areas, you'll soon find purity growing in your life.

Purity of the mind: *"I will set no worthless thing before my eyes"* (Ps. 101:3, NASB).

Did you know that when you surf the Net, the pictures appearing on your screen are saved in a temporary Internet folder on your hard drive? If you know where to look, you can actually go in and see all the little buttons and advertising strips. By the way, you can see everything else you look at, too. The same is true with your mind. Whatever you allow in through your eyes is permanently recorded in your mind.

The next time you're surfing the Net or the T.V., and you come to "that channel," I pray you'll hear God say, "What's the matter, can't you push the button one more time?"

Purity of the heart: *"A perverse heart shall depart from me. I will know no evil"* (Ps. 101:4, NASB).

Our heart motives determine what we do. Even our unconscious choices are made out of our motives. A perverse heart is full of selfish and impure motives. It will dilute our passion for God and will ultimately lead us to make faulty, impure choices. Each of us must monitor our heart for the motives that move us.

Purity of Words: *"Whoever secretly slanders his neighbor, him will I destroy"* (Ps. 101:5, NASB).

King David tells us that words have the power to promote purity both in our own lives and in the lives of those around us. How many times have you been in a room where one of your friends is being nice to someone, and when that person leaves they talk badly about them? They are two-faced. Their nice words are a front to the slander that follows. Words must be used wisely.

> **From what do you need to protect your mind?**
>
> **How will you do it?**
>
> *What are your motives for fame, romance, and money?*

Take the following challenge to see if you use words to do more *hurting* or more *healing*.

In the following situations, to what degree are you more likely to use words that hurt or words that heal? Circle one of the numbers in each situation.

	More Hurting						More Healing
When I talk with my parents	4	3	2	1	2	3	4
Boyfriend/Girlfriend conflict	4	3	2	1	2	3	4
The lady in the registrar's office	4	3	2	1	2	3	4
Roommate	4	3	2	1	2	3	4
The drive-through window guy	4	3	2	1	2	3	4
My psychic connection	4	3	2	1	2	3	4

Purity in relationships

David makes it clear about the people he will associate with...and those he won't associate with.

"Whoever secretly slanders his neighbor, him I will destroy; No one who has a haughty look and an arrogant heart will I endure....He who practices deceit shall not dwell within my house; He who speaks falsehood shall not maintain his position before me" (Ps. 101:5, 7, NASB).

It is vital to our purity that we carefully choose the people we allow closest to us. The character of the people we allow closest to us is more important than the way they look or where they come from. **The character each one chooses serves to influence the character of others.**

The Scripture gives us a list of cautions that can help protect purity in our relationships. Be careful when you see people with these character traits:

A haughty look. (Psalm 101:5*b*) This person has a prideful, arrogant attitude and appearance. Haughty people very often have their own agenda and will use you to accomplish it.

Anyone who practices deceit. (Psalm 101:7) This person purposely deceives others. If they deceive others, chances are, they will sooner or later deceive you.

Anyone who speaks falsehood. (Psalm 101:7) This person frequently lies and shades the truth. Why would you want to be with anyone who doesn't tell the truth?

Our earliest understanding of purity probably was learned from our parents and grandparents. Positive or negative, it's important to know what they've taught us.

The Bible is so practical to your everyday life. God tells us to look for friends who have these character traits:

Faithful. (Ps. 101:6) These people do what they say they will do. They support you to your face *and* behind your back.

Those whose walk is blameless. (Ps. 101:6) These people understand the importance of making sure their own lives are on track and are positive examples for others.

The people you allow closest to you directly impact the power purity produces in your life. David knew that the relationships he chose either built or destroyed his personal purity. He chose to limit the influences of his life by developing relationships with those people who would positively impact his purity.

Purity is more than a signed pledge card or a ring or pendant you wear. **Purity is a choice you make every day.** Purity comes out of a positive, passionate relationship with God. We choose purity when our motives come out of love for the One who loves us most.

Biblical purity runs through my thoughts, my words, and my actions.

One thing that really sticks with me that my grandparents taught me about purity is...

If I could choose one thing I admire most about my mom and dad, it would be...

My friends at school see me as. . .

Between You and God

These questions are provided to help you pry open areas of your life to apply the truths of this session.

In 1 Timothy 4:12 Paul reminds us that we are to set an example in five areas of our lives, including purity. What are some areas that come to mind when you think of purity?

Why do you think it is important for you to set an example in purity?

Living a life of purity is difficult for me because

A person who has been a specific example to me in the area of purity is

Suppose a person has already failed to be pure in a sexual relationship. How can a fresh start be made? Is such a person to be considered "damaged goods" forever? Why or why not?

Why does it appear difficult for some Christians to forgive a sexual sin?

How do you respond when someone in a group begins to tell a "dirty" joke?
[ ] I walk away.
[ ] I tell them to shut up.
[ ] I change the subject.
[ ] I laugh with them.
[ ] I do nothing.
[ ] Or _____

the seeds of self-destruction

Start with Christ, who lives in you.

Identify the seeds of self-destruction.

Manage your thought life.

Plan your personal convictions.

Live by design.

Exchange wrong decisions for right ones.

The Seeds of Self-Destruction

Idolized by thousands of young adults, Chris Farley had reached the pinnacle of entertainment success. Few people could make us laugh the way he did. Throughout his short-lived career, Chris Farley planted deadly seeds that would lead to his own destruction and a huge loss to the entertainment industry.

Solomon, King of Israel, was the world's wisest and most wealthy man. People came to him to get his insight on what was happening in their world. They brought him incredibly valuable gifts along with all the respect anybody in the world could ever want.

Solomon thought he was invincible. He thought his life was so blessed that nothing could separate him from his success. This was the man who wrote the Proverbs, the wisest literature ever written. This was the man who had the wisdom, the power, and the wealth. Yet he blew it.

How could a man with all this in his favor blow it? The same way some of our modern day folk heroes do. He made decisions that began to sow the seeds of self-destruction deep into his life.

List the things you value most in life. (talents, traits, etc.)

_____   _____

_____   _____

_____   _____

What are the areas of your life you have the most confidence in?

_____   _____

_____   _____

_____   _____

The seeds of self-destruction tend to be most fertile when they are planted in the areas of our value, success, and confidence. During the rest of this session, keep in mind that these could be the areas of your life where you are most vulnerable to self-destruction.

Seed One:
POSITIVE DECEPTION
"It's not going to happen to me."

We have all been tricked into something that on the surface looked innocent, only later to find that the core of what looked "innocent" was really dark and perverted. King Solomon married many foreign women and allowed them to bring their religions into his home. He believed that he could marry these women and allow them to continue their religious practices without bringing any harm to himself or his country. He had no intention of worshipping their gods, nor did he have any intention for his countrymen to worship them.

Solomon was deceived by his own perceived ability to control himself and the influences he allowed into his home and his country. By overestimating his ability to control the influence, he fell prey to the positive deception.

We think we can allow a small compromise in a strong area of our lives. If it gets out of hand, we think it's easily stopped. These compromises produce open rebellion against God's principles for our lives. At first we naively think we can turn around. Only after we are in too far do we find ourselves being willfully led to our own destruction.

The seeds of positive deception can sound like many of the things we hear every day. Do any of these sound familiar?

"I'll do this first, and then I'll come back to God."
"It's all in good fun."
"But I really love this person."
"If I stay with them, I can change them."
"It's not really hurting anybody."
"I need to experience this."
"I still believe in God."
"What I'm doing is not really wrong."

"If they can, why can't I?"
"If you only knew what I've been through."
"They're good people."

The problem is, we don't finish these sentences. Behind each of these sentences is a big "even though..."
"...even though I know it's not wise."
"...even though I know it could harm me."
"...even though they don't believe in God."
"...even though I will have to compromise to do it."
"...even though it may hurt me in the long run."
"...even though I already know the truth."
"...even though I'm not acting like it."
"...even though God does not approve of it."
"...even though I'm a Christian and should live by a different standard."
"...even though the truth is still the truth no matter what my situation."
"...even though they don't believe what I believe."

Take a minute to read back through the "...even though" list above and put a mark by the "...even though" phrases you have used. When did you use them? Why did you choose to use them?

Now take another few minutes to remember the negative consequences you experienced after making those choices. Want to do it again? I think not.

> **Here's the essence of the first seed of self-destruction:**
>
> *I am deceived when I believe that my good intentions will decrease the negative consequences of my actions.*

Seed Two: PERSONAL DECISION
"I know what God has said, but I don't care."

This seed has two parts: It is *specific* and *willful.*

First, the personal decision is *specific.*
In an attempt to avoid personal responsibility, we say, "I don't know what got into me." By refusing to be specific about our choices, we continue to allow the seed to grow and take root in that area of our lives.
In verse 1 of 1 Kings 11, the Bible tells us that King Solomon loved many foreign women. His love was a specific choice.

We make choices for ourselves; no one makes them for us. When we willfully turn away from what God has told us, we have made a personal decision to basically ignore God. We think we can do whatever we want, and God isn't big enough to do anything about it.

I heard an incredible news story about college football players betting against their own team. The NCAA was investigating these players for not only betting that their team would lose, but intentionally fumbling the ball. These young men each made a personal decision to put their own desires above the goals of the team. No one made them make this choice. Their personal decisions not only sacrificed the team's goals, a great deal of self-destruction entered their own lives.

The choice to sow the seed of self-destruction is always specific. For Solomon, it came in the area of relationships. For you, it might be different. The seed of destruction is always specific, not vague.

Here are some areas where the seed of self-destruction might be planted. At least one of yours is on the list.

- **Pride**—thinking that I'm above falling for any temptation.
- **Independence**—forgetting that accountability is vital to my personal purity.
- **Overconfidence**—believing that I make it happen with my talents and abilities.
- **Control**—failing to understand my own choices are all I can control.
- **Money**—believing that I can serve both money and God.
- **Power**—thinking that God shares His.
- **Lust**—forgetting that it's the same as adultery.
- **False sense of spirituality**—believing that my works are my righteousness.

I was in Louisiana speaking at a CrossSeekers conference. After I finished speaking, a sophomore coed came up to me and thanked me for what I had to say, but then said something I hear all the time after I speak. "Dave," she said, "all the things you told us tonight are things I'm already doing. I've got all that together. In fact, I learned everything there was to know about living the Christian life by the time I was 13." She was serious. I moved back a step or two and said to her, "Would you mind if we stand a little further apart, you know, just in case of lightning?"

I hear this profession of false spirituality all the time. It comes mostly from students who have grown up in church. Many of them have gone to Christian schools. There's nothing wrong with church or Christian

> *Before moving on, take a moment to write out a prayer to God asking Him to help you stay humble and vulnerable to His leadership, and that He will show you where you may have allowed this seed of self-destruction to be planted. If you are still unaware of the area of your life most open to this attack, ask God to reveal that to you.*

schools. There is definitely something wrong with anyone believing the lie that they have their Christian life all together. This is a lifelong process. The apostle Paul, perhaps the one Christian who had more of it together than any of us said, *"Not that I have already attained it, or have already become perfect..."* (Phil. 3:12, NASB).

Take this solemn warning from 1 Corinthians 10:12: *"Therefore let him who thinks he stands take heed lest he fall"* (NIV).

Second, the personal decision is *willful*.
In 1 Kings 11:2, Solomon was told not to associate with these women because they would turn his heart from God. Solomon held fast to his choice to love these women, and the result was unnecessary pain and destruction.

God provides each of us with the specific warning that is strong enough to get our attention. He loves us and wants His best for our lives. He knows that we don't have to make choices that will plant destructive seeds in our lives. He doesn't want us to willfully pursue the choices that will lead to our destruction, so He gives each of us adequate warning.

This is a personal challenge to do something about your willful choices instead of settling into them like a fat guy in a hammock after a tub of chunky chocolate ice cream. You have a choice.

We have each followed after what we want. Perhaps you are saying, "I'd like to make the move back to God and have Him remove those seeds of self-destruction." You must come back to the self-awareness of your sin before God can begin to replant *His seed* in your life.

Take a moment and identify the seeds of sin in your life. What are the willful, purposeful sins of self-destruction you have chosen? Write them in the seeds below.

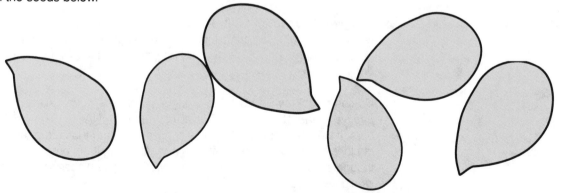

Now ask God to plant His seeds in your life. In the seeds below, write the things you would like God to plant in place of the sin seeds.

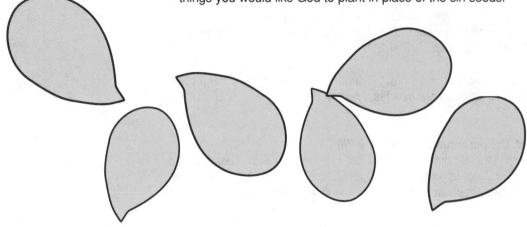

Seed Three:
PROGRESSIVE DECAY
"Hey, I know when to stop."

In 1 Kings 11, verses 3-4, the Scripture tells us that Solomon's wives turned his heart away from God. Solomon had underestimated his ability to stand firm. He made his choice contrary to God's expressed will.

Compromise doesn't happen all at once. If it did, we wouldn't make most of the compromises we do. We are smart enough not to pay someone $10,000 to infect our lungs with cancer. Yet after smoking five packs a week for 20 years, we will spend more than that for the same effect. We just think it won't happen to us.

It begins as a thought. When it came to his 700 wives and concubines, Solomon thought, "I'll bring them into my kingdom, I'll win them to my God, I'll change them." We say, "It'll be just one night." "I'll go, but I won't drink."

It's controllable while it's still a thought. *"...We are taking every thought captive to the obedience of Christ"* (2 Cor. 10:5, NASB). The choice is ours. If we don't take our thoughts captive, we learn to tolerate them. It's not long before we justify them so we can live with them emotionally. Our thoughts lead us to make decisions lowering us to places we swore we would never be.

Without careful examination of your own life, you will not be able to eliminate these destructive seeds.

diary of decay

Think of a specific problem area of your life. What seems to be the first step in your decay?

Who was with you?

What prompted you to think these thoughts?

These are questions to help you identify and deal with the seeds of destruction you have planted in your life.

It results in personal failure. See 1 Kings 11:6. Solomon did what was evil. *He did not follow the Lord fully.* Solomon built high places of worship to the gods of his wives. The man who had built a most glorious temple to the Living God now found himself using his power and prosperity to build high places of worship to the false gods he had come to tolerate. The once great king Solomon now found himself in bondage to things he never though possible.

diary of decay

How did your thought(s) lead to action(s)?

Was it quick or slow?

What were the steps that led to the action?

What can you learn from this?

diary of decay

How were you trapped by this?

What did it cost you physically, emotionally, spiritually?

What did it cost others?

What were the internal consequences?

You can trace every compromise back through these three things: THOUGHT, ACTION, BONDAGE.

It produces inescapable bondage. Continuing with our story found in 1 Kings 11:7-8, Solomon built these high places of worship east of Jerusalem, where the Mount of Olives is. The Bible says he built these altars for all his wives who burned incense and sacrificed to their gods. There must have been a considerable amount of smoke going up each day from these altars. And Solomon had the best seat in the house. He could look out his window and watch the incense as it went up.

Solomon had made the kingdom his father had given him immeasurably wealthy. The wars his father had fought gave Solomon the opportunity to make the land secure beyond understanding. The wall of Jerusalem was strong, and the people felt secure. But no one saw the inescapable bondage choking the spiritual life out of the people and their king. Idolatry became Israel's bondage.

Personal decision produces destruction.

When you compromise, you take God on personally...one on one. Solomon knew what God required, yet he chose to do his own will. He basically looked into the face of God and said, "I know what You told me to do, but I don't think You're big enough to do anything about it." That's pretty blunt, but when we know the truth of God and disregard it because we think we know better, it's just the same as telling God He's not big enough to do anything about it.

The seeds of self-destruction will bear fruit in our lives. But they can be rooted out and dealt with before the permanent damage is done. If you choose to leave the seeds planted and not uproot them, several consequences will result.

Three guaranteed consequences:

1. God deals with us. See 1 Kings 11:9-11. The Lord was angry and took the kingdom away from Solomon and gave it to another. Solomon found out that it's impossible to defy the principles of God and still benefit from His promises. God's promises are filled with blessings that are only realized when we live in His principles. *"For he who does wrong will receive the consequences of the wrong which he has done, and that without partiality"* (Col. 3:25, NASB).

2. It will catch up with you. Read 1 Kings 11:14. The Lord raised up an adversary for Solomon. Until this time, no one dared face Solomon and his power. This was only because God's benefits and blessings rested on Solomon. Because of Solomon's choices, God raised up an enemy for Solomon. It wasn't enough that idolatry was commonplace in the kingdom, now Solomon would begin to personally feel the loss of God's blessing.

3. Life becomes counterproductive. See 1 Kings 11:11. *"I will surely tear the kingdom from you"* (NASB). There came a point in Solomon's life that regardless of how much or how hard he worked to continue to build his kingdom, it was all counterproductive. Perhaps there has come a time in your life when it didn't seem to matter how hard you worked at something, that nothing good would come of it. If so, you can relate with Solomon's self-imposed position.

The one option God provided Solomon is the same option He provides us when we realize that we have sown the seeds of self-destruction and are now living in their fruit. **What is needed is to repent and return to God.**

To make things right, we must repent and return to God.
If Solomon, Samson, David, or Judas came and sat in your Bible study, they would say the same thing, "Repent and return to God before it's too late." Every one of them had a time when they thought, "I need to get out of this before it's too late!" If you could only hear the urgency in their voices, you would stop right now.

If you're ready to repent and return to God, pray the suggested simple prayer on the following page to help.

Dear God,

I have willfully chosen my own way over Your way. I have known Your will and have decided to do something different. I really thought I knew better than You. I thought I could handle it. I thought I could have my way and still live in the benefits and blessings You promised me. I was wrong. I allowed myself to be deceived. I know the personal destruction I have brought on myself, and I need You to rescue me from the bondage I have chosen. I confess my sin and repent and return to You. Please completely uproot the seeds of self-destruction I have planted in my life and plant deep within me Your seeds of character, that I may grow into the person You want me to become.

Between You and God

These questions are provided to help you pry open areas of your life to apply the truths of this session.

Recall a recent example in your life when you really sensed the planting of "seeds of self-destruction" in one or more of the following areas (see page 26):

[ ] Pride
[ ] Independence
[ ] Overconfidence
[ ] Control
[ ] Money
[ ] Power
[ ] Lust
[ ] False sense of spirituality

What ambition in your life hurts you more than it helps? Identify it here.

In what area of your life do you constantly delude yourself? Identify it here.

Some may reason that since Jesus said that lusting is committing adultery in the heart (Matt.5:28), it wouldn't be any worse to go "all the way." How would you respond to such reasoning? Jot down two responses.

1.

2.

How would you lovingly deal with a Christian who honestly does not see any wrong in a homosexual relationship? Describe it in the space below.

mental floss

Start with Christ, who lives in you.
Identify the seeds of self-destruction.
Manage your thought life.
Plan your personal convictions.
Live by design.
Exchange wrong decisions for right ones.

Mental Floss

Not long ago, I was in Atlanta to speak at a conference. One afternoon when the conference was over, a youth minister friend of mine invited me over to his house for dinner. You need to understand something about me. I really don't like going over to people's houses, and I like even less eating when I get there. But here I was doing both of these things which I so desperately dislike.

As I drove through the neighborhood and up to the house, I noticed house after house that looked identical—two cars, neatly trimmed yards, you know, very *Children of the Corn*-ish. Well, I parked, walked up to the door, rang the bell, and was greeted by a house full of couples about my age, along with their children.

My friend invited me out to the deck while he cooked. He introduced me around to everyone and I gave my seven-minute prepared speech. "Hi, I'm Dave Edwards. I speak in churches, do Bible studies, blah, blah, blah." Then I just listened as the rest of the couples talked about their children. Spencer's first tooth...Katelin's first step, you know the bit. They were all laughing and enjoying themselves when suddenly, the conversation stopped, and everyone looked at me.

I didn't know what to say. I'm not married, and I don't have any nieces or nephews to talk about their teeth or the first step. I was just sitting there grinding on my burger, trying to think of something to say. I was the guest of honor. I had to say something, and it had better be good.

So I swallowed the bite I was working on, cleared my throat and said, "I got a new pair of shoes."

No one knew what to say. My brilliant attempt at conversation was met with a clumsy silence that made everyone uncomfortable. Needless to say, I said very little the rest of the evening.

After dinner, I left the party and drove back to the motel thinking about the couples I had just embarrassed myself in front of. These people were my age, and they had families, homes, and children. And me...well, I struggle just keeping up with my motel room key. All this really got to me.

That event ignited a brushfire of negative thoughts like, "What am I doing with my life?" "Is what I'm doing really all that valuable?" "I feel really dumb." "Where do I really fit in?" These destructive thoughts began to take hold, and I knew I had to do something.

I knew that if I left these thoughts unchecked, they would begin to shape my reality, my self-perception, and ultimately what God can do in and through me. I learned a long time ago that I am responsible for choosing the thoughts controlling my mind. I am responsible for weeding out the destructive thoughts, and I am responsible for cultivating the healthy thoughts.

When we choose to listen to destructive thoughts, it causes depression. But when we choose to replace these destructive thoughts with God's thoughts, we become stronger and more useable to God.

"'For I know the plans that I have for you,' declares the LORD, 'plans for welfare and not for calamity to give you a future and a hope'" (Jer. 29:11, NASB).

This whole situation sparked a brushfire of negative thoughts. The only way that fire can be extinguished and life can begin again is to enter into the process of renewing your mind. When we are enticed to believe negative thoughts about our design and destiny, we must look at the Word of God.

Here's what we must remember in the midst of struggle:
• I am chosen in Christ.
• God has called me in a special way.
• God has gifted me to do everything He has called me to do.
• God has given me a specific niche to fill in His kingdom.

And besides that, there's not an auditorium large enough to hold the people who would come to my funeral!

Reading the Word of God is vital; it gives us God's viewpoint about our lives. It is sometimes more important to read the Word of God than it is to pray, because you can spend time praying and never get to reading. When you start with the Word, it will cause you to pray through what you are reading. When it comes to flossing out old ways of thinking, reading the Word of God is our only offensive weapon.

If you are a believer, Jesus Christ lives in you. When you go to the Bible for help and guidance, the Spirit of God connects with the Word of God, and there is synergy. These two are meant to work together. *"But when He, the Spirit of truth, comes, He will guide you into all the truth; for He will not speak on His own initiative, but whatever He hears, He will speak; and He will disclose to you what is to come"* (John 16:13, NASB).

I want to show you how the Word of God functions as mental floss for our minds. It is the perfect agent to get between those hard-to-reach places and clean out the destructive thoughts that keep us from being and becoming all God has in store for us.

"For the word of God is living and active and sharper than any two-edged sword, and piercing as far as the division of soul and spirit, of both joints and marrow, and able to judge the thoughts and intentions of the heart" (Hebrews 4:12, NASB).

This chapter has two main points: **The role of God's Word** and **the reality of God's Word.**

THE ROLE OF GOD'S WORD

The Antidote to Temptation

"Then Jesus was led up by the Spirit...to be tempted by the devil" (Matt. 4:1, NASB).

Scripture is the only effective antidote for temptation. The Scripture dilutes the effects of the temptation on our minds and makes it resistible. The Word of God helps us be more than conquerors in the face of temptation.

Here's how Jesus used the Word when He faced temptations.
In Matthew 4:1-11, the Spirit of God led Jesus into the wilderness to be tempted by Satan. When Satan came to Jesus, he dared Him to prove He had all the messianic power. If Jesus had made bread out of stones, jumped off the temple, or bowed down and worshipped Satan, He would have fallen for the trap. But Jesus applied the antidote of Scripture. The same is true when we face temptation; the Word of God keeps us from falling for every temptation that is thrown at us.

> **The Word of God is the only thing that will keep you out of sin—and as you understand and apply the Word, you won't give in to temptation.**

Three Basic Areas of Temptation

"For all that is in the world, the lust of the flesh and the lust of the eyes and the boastful pride of life, is not from the Father, but is from the world" (1 John 2:16, NASB). There are basically three areas of temptations. They are:
1. EROTIC—using people or things to satisfy our basic instincts.
2. ENVY—wanting something you don't want the other person to have.
3. EGO—wanting to impress someone by being someone you're not.

What are the subtle ways these are played out in your life?

Write your answers to the following:

I wanted something so badly that the envy made me...

I feel the need to impress others when...

I had a crush on this person because I liked...

One of the Scriptures that has helped me fight temptation is...

The Arsenal of Truth
Matthew 4:3-4, 6-7, 9-10 *"...it is written"* (NASB).

The priority in Jesus' life was the Word of God. Jesus could have said anything in response to the temptations, and it would have been the Word of God. Instead, He quoted the Old Testament. There was a time in Jesus' life when He purposefully planted the Word of God deep in His mind so it would be there to draw out when He needed it.

The Word of God was more than Jesus' devotional material; it was His bread of life. Jesus heard His Father in the pages of Scripture. He had left everything to come to earth. The intimacy He had left behind in heaven was found as He fed on God's Word. We need to see the time we interact with the Word of God as an investment in intimacy.

The time to make these investments is every day. You don't know what battle you'll find staring you in the face next. It will be too late when the next struggle is right up on you. The time to prepare to win is before the drink is offered. The preparation to win out over the temptation to cheat comes before realizing you don't know the answers on a test. Prepare to win over lust before the buttons fly. The daily investments you make in becoming intimate with God's Word will show up when it really counts.

Every time Satan said, "if," Jesus responded with, "it is written." For every lie Satan fired at Him, Jesus had a corresponding truth. How many, "it is writtens" do you know? If you were in the desert being tempted by Satan's "ifs," how many scriptural answers would you know? How many "it is writtens" do you have in your arsenal?

Is your arsenal of truth well stocked?

The agent of transformation

"...then the devil left Him" (Matt. 4:11, NASB).

The process of transformation is taking out the old and putting in the new.

God is in the process of transforming you into the image of Jesus Christ. *Transformation* means change. We can't change ourselves into Christ's image; we must **be** changed by something. God's Word is the agent of transformation. *"And do not be conformed to this world, but be transformed by the renewing of your mind, that you may prove what the will of God is, that which is good and acceptable and perfect"* (Rom. 12:2, NASB).

Every time you are tempted, it's an opportunity for God to lead you past the obstacle and into further personal transformation. God wants you transformed into Christ's image, so expect obstacles.

Here's a Christian maturity secret: **The battle of the Christian's life is won or lost in the theatre of your mind.** Second Corinthians 10:4-6 tells us that the weapons of our warfare are spiritual weapons. We are fighting an unseen enemy. Our enemy doesn't dig his foxholes in dirt, he digs them in the minds of men. Our enemy's battle plan is not to control a city, but to control our minds.

Real progress in the Christian life is made when our thinking starts to change. Our thinking starts to change when we regularly apply the Word of God to our minds. The Word of God is the agent producing God's goal of your transformation.

THE REALITY OF GOD'S WORD

In John 8:31-32, Jesus reveals how the truth of God's Word becomes real in our lives in three ways.

The fight for truth

"If you abide in My word, then you are truly disciples of Mine; and you shall know the truth, and the truth shall make you free" (John 8:31b-32, NASB).

The fight for truth is between our emotions and the Word of God. We enter into this world being led by our emotions. When we're hurt, we cry. When we're hungry, we scream. And when we're happy, we laugh. This is normal for children, but too many of us allow our emotions to continue as the leader of our adult lives.

God gave emotions to serve as sensors. They enable us to enjoy a situation, experience a moment, and interpret dangers. Our emotions are the feelers of our lives. They were never meant to lead.

Emotions are real, but not always right.

When truth is introduced into a life that has been led by emotions, there is a fight. When someone who has struggled with forgiveness is told, "God has forgiven you and will never bring that up again," they respond with, "Maybe so, but I don't feel forgiven." They believe emotions over truth.

When emotions lead, they will justify whatever the mind is thinking. The mind says, "No one understands you," and our emotions justify this by making us feel isolated. Our thoughts whisper, "You're the only one who has ever gone through this," and the emotions kick in by making us feel weird, hopeless, and victimized.

Ladies! Maybe you have heard this in your thought life: "That outfit makes you look huge!" Your emotions punctuate the chorus with, "What a pig! You'd better just stay behind your desk."

From society or family, we have been bombarded with thoughts like, "You won't be happy until you're married." "You have to act and look a certain way to fit in." Our emotions take thoughts like these and make us feel desperate and insecure.

Letting emotions lead causes us to misinterpret the events of our lives. When emotions are the lenses through which everything is viewed, it's impossible to get an accurate read on anything. **Letting emotions control will force the Word of God to become subjective.** Because we have chosen emotions to be the basis of reality, we believe that if we violate how we feel, it must not be real.

The fight for truth is to reverse the emotional control. When the truth of God is planted in the mind, it begins to leak out into the habits, actions, and events of our lives. As we allow the Word of God to take the lead in our lives, our emotions will come to obey the truth. Over time, we will find that our lives take on a healthy emotional balance, because truth has won the fight, and we are no longer wackos.

The Framework of Truth

"And you shall know the truth..." (John 8:32, NASB).

Simply put, *THE TRUTH* is God's Word, not what people say about God's Word, or what you can read about God's Word. The truth is the Spirit-breathed Word of God.

The Word of God is the basis for our faith and the Word gives us faith. Faith, in turn, helps us overcome whatever we face.

The Word of God is the framework that everything else is hung on. The Word of God is the basis for the ethics of our lives. You have been given the privilege to know the truth and be free. The word "know" in John 8:32 means that you can live out the Word of God in your everyday life with the highest conviction and belief that you have confidently chosen that which is right.

"I will walk within my house in the integrity of my heart" (Ps. 101:2, NASB).

These six things are the basics of kingdom ethics. Read the verses listed and begin now to establish God's Word as the foundation for your ethics.

• Justice	Deuteronomy 16:19
• Holiness	Ephesians 4:24
• Love	Luke 6:32-35
• Purity	1 Corinthians 16:19-20
• Service	Colossians 3:22
• Righteousness	Philippians 3:9

Ask yourself, "How do these ethics form the framework of truth for my life?"

> **You don't fight thoughts with thoughts, you fight thoughts with words.**

The function of truth

"...and the truth shall make you free" (John 8:32, NIV).

The function of truth is to make you FREE.

Any place in our lives we believe a lie is a place where the truth is not. The place we find ourselves in bondage to destructive behavior is a place where truth needs to be applied. Where there is truth, there is freedom—freedom to live the full and meaningful life Jesus promised in John 10:10b, *"I came that they might have life, and might have it abundantly"* (NASB).

For the truth to free us, it requires us to make an intentional choice to begin the process of renewing our minds. The process is simple; the journey is not. **The process begins when you recognize a lie and respond with the truth.**

Here is a quick list of Scripture truths. Take a few moments to recognize the lies, read the truths in the Scriptures, and then write the Scriptures in your own words.

"FOR EVERY LIE, THERE'S A CORRESPONDING TRUTH."

Lie	Truth	Your own words
"It's too late for me to start over."	Psalm 138:8	
"I have a right to get even."	Romans 12:17	
"I can do it myself. No one will tell me what to do."	Psalm 118:6,9	
"You gotta do what it takes to fit in."	Proverbs 13:20	
"Not even God can get me out of this one."	Romans 8:28	
"I can't."	Philippians 4:13	
"It's my life. I'll do what I want to."	Proverbs 3:5-6	
"I can't help it. It's just the way I am."	2 Corinthians 10:5	
"My life is one big mistake."	Psalm 139:14-15	
"Character doesn't matter."	Proverbs 10:9	

These and many other verses throughout the Scripture are our most powerful weapons against temptation. Choose the ones that benefit you the most and write them out on index cards to carry with you. Then begin the process of memorizing them, meditating on them, and mouthing (or speaking) them out loud in your specific situations. With practice, these powerful weapons become lethal to temptation.

Pick one of the verses from the preceding text and write it in your own words; then memorize it and make it your own.

"He who loves purity of heart and whose speech is gracious, the king is his friend" (Prov. 22:11, NASB).

Conclusion

Something is going to shape our lives. We get to choose. It will either be the lies we've grown up believing, the messages of the world, or the truth of God. The good news is, it's not too late to begin the process of renewing your mind with the Word of God.

Make daily Bible reading a habit. Allow God's Word to be the mental floss to get into those hard-to-reach places and root out the lies you have chosen to believe. Allow God's Word to transform your mind. As you do, you will find that it is renewing your thinking, your words, and ultimately your choices.

Between You and God

These questions are provided to help you pry open areas of your life to apply the truths of this session.

When did the Bible come to mean more to you than just another book?

The Word of God is essential in preparing to win over temptation. What is your plan for putting the Word into your life?

Long range plan

Plan for this year

Daily actions

Memorization

Recall the first verse of Scripture you memorized. Write it here. How has it helped you?

What verse or passage of Scripture best defines your life purpose?

If you spent six hours a day practicing tennis, and one hour a week practicing golf, which would you most likely be better at? If you spent six hours a day watching movies and TV, and one hour a week reading the Bible, which one would be winning the battle for your mind?

What decisions should you make *before* going to a party where alcohol and drugs will be available? (hint: Look at Genesis 39:2-10 and Daniel 1:8.)

What are some of the prevalent temptations for you on the college campus?

Memorize 1 Corinthians 10:13 and trust the Lord to bring it to mind when you face temptation. Quote it to yourself as you surf the Net, rent a video, or peruse a magazine.

how to be a person
people want to be with

Start with Christ, who lives in you.
    Identify the seeds of self-destruction.
    Manage your thought life.
      Plan your personal convictions.
        Live by design.
          Exchange wrong decisions for right ones.

How to Be a Person People Want to Be With

Here's a list of people we can all do without.

Power-hungry politicians

Politicians with the Dockers down around their ankles. Where's the real character of leadership? In the courts and in the capital, no one wants to lower the gavel and call it what it is: a lack of character. Politicians have taught us that if you cheat, lie, and vilify, one day you could be elected President. The lack of character is tearing our country apart like a rock band at a posh hotel.

Ungrateful athletes

There was a time when sports were played by heroes on a field of honor, and the ethic was "work hard, play fair, become a hero, give back to the fans, and ride off into the sunset." But now, the ethic of athletes is, "Do crack, beat your wife, become a felon, get paroled, and drive a Porsche off into the sunset." Today, athletes have become as fake as their polyester uniforms.

Bitter bag boys

Not long ago I was in a grocery store standing in the express lane. The cashier was friendly enough; she even smiled as I handed her the $13.74. I had just a few items lying at the end of the counter, and was about to bag them myself when a wrinkled white shirt with a 17-year old boy inside said, "Hey, that's my job!" This guy had to play pick-up basketball in his apartment complex. He started slam-dunking each of my grocery items into one of the flimsy plastic bags. I looked at him and wondered when was the last time he washed his face or ironed his shirt. He slammed the last item (a package of Twizzlers) into the bag, jerked the bag off the counter, and shoved it at me. I asked him, "Isn't there anything you'd like to say to me...like maybe, 'Thank you?'" He turned to leave, and without even looking at me, he said, "It says it on the bag!"

People who talk in movie theaters

…you know what I mean.

I have friends who are great people. I go to dinner and shopping with them. But you get them in a movie theater, the lights go out, and they start asking me questions about the movie. I'm confused. Did I get there before they did?

People with notions of entitlement

Yes, you do have the *right* to remain silent, but also you have the *responsibility* to not scream in a restaurant. You have the *right* to free speech, but also you have the *responsibility* not to speak so loudly that I hear your dinner conversation three tables away.

People on daytime T.V. talk shows

A large part of America hardly notices the people who parade into their living rooms on the average daytime T.V. talk show. These people have more baggage than an American Airlines Skycap. The security guards run on the stage when a 240-pound man hits his 110-pound girlfriend because she stole his Skoal. We used to reserve the word "famous" for people who did outstanding or extraordinary things. Now almost anyone can have their 15 minutes of fame. The weirder, the better. We used to admire the character of famous people. Now we take delight in the crudity of freaks. What Americans have forgotten is that the things that matter in the trailer park, don't matter in the real world. We give our permission for the unqualified to speak for the uninformed.

Those who have just forgotten the basic rules of civility

People get on each other's nerves because we've forgotten the basic rules of civility: Don't clip your fingernails in a restaurant. Cover your mouth when you cough. Step away from the table when you blow your nose. And make sure you're not standing by someone else's table. Don't burp so loudly that everyone turns around and looks at you. Don't honk at the old lady just because she crosses the street slowly. Have your money ready in the grocery store line and, oh yeah, count your items before getting into the 12-or-less line.

Hulks in health clubs

See the people on a steroid feast. Health clubs are filled with people who can bench press motorcycles. They wear out treadmills and then go eat a super-sized happy snack. Some of the guys have arms so big they can't button their own pants.

As a nation, we've spent so much time working on our bodies that we've forgotten to work on our souls. We would rather look at the man in the mirror than take a long, hard look *into* the man in the mirror.

Look around you. It's easier to find people you don't want to be with than it is people you do. Now take a look at the people who are looking at you. Would they want to be with you? Are you a person people want to be with?

Psalm 24 tells us how to be a person people want to be with. It also tells us the kind of person God wants to be with. People want to be with other people who have character. People want to be with people who do more than shop right; they want to be with people whose insides match their outsides.

This is a struggle we all recognize. We all have parts of our lives that make it difficult for others to want to be around us. So here we are in Session 4, learning how to develop the purity of Christ in us.

The process begins on the inside. It's not as easy as swallowing a pill or getting an injection of new personality. God wants to literally remake you from the inside out. (Here's proof: Philippians 2:13.) There are two ways to change the shape of an ice cube. You can hit it with a hammer and refreeze it in a new mold. Or you can melt the ice cube, pour it into the new mold, and then refreeze it. Both ways are effective, but the first way is not very subtle, and it causes a lot of waste. When it comes to God's remake of you, you'll be glad to know God uses the second method. With the warmth of His love, He melts your heart so you can adapt to the changes He is bringing about from the inside out.

There are three things that must happen for us to develop the purity of Christ in our lives.

1. ADAPT TO THE MORAL ATTRIBUTES OF GOD.

"Who may ascend into the hill of the Lord? Or who may stand in His holy place? He who has clean hands and a pure heart, who has not lifted up his soul to falsehood, and has not sworn deceitfully. He shall receive a blessing from the Lord and righteousness from the God of his salvation" (Ps. 24:3-5, NASB).

David was asking God, "Who gets to be with You?" The answer is, he who has clean hands.

Clean hands

David was a man who knew how God acted. The clean hands he referred to are the moral attributes of God. When we repent and ask Jesus to be our Lord and Savior, He makes us clean. Every moral attribute of God is given to us when Jesus comes into our lives.

Even though God has placed His attributes in us, they don't come activated.

It's like one of those Chia pets people give for Christmas (sing it if you know it… "cha,cha,cha,chi-a"). The dirt and seeds come shipped already inside the pottery. The pottery needs to be soaked in water to activate the seeds. If you don't add water, all you'll have is an ugly piece of pottery. Come to think of it, even if you do add water, all you'll have is an ugly, fuzzy piece of pottery. God's moral attributes are already inside you. But you have to adapt to the attributes.

There are four attributes we must conform our lives to:

Holiness

Holiness

Holiness is complete oneness in purpose and will. To God, holiness means that He is absolutely committed to His will. He is completely committed to accomplishing His will in your life. God tells us to *"Be holy for I am holy"* (Lev. 11:45, NASB). He means that we are to be committed to His will as He is.

> You adapt to holiness by asking, "What does God want?"

> The more you choose to bend your will to the perfect will of God, the more character of holiness comes out through you.

We grow in holiness as we adapt to the will of God. It's a process that takes a lifetime and is never fully finished. God's will is perfect and complete, and He reveals to us only what we are prepared to handle. God doesn't hide His will like carefully hidden Easter eggs. He makes plain to anyone who genuinely seeks to follow Him. Choose to follow God's will before He reveals it.

Righteousness

God is righteous. **This means He hates evil and blesses good.** Righteousness is the way God acts in and through our lives. It changes who we are and why we do what we do. The blueprint of righteousness is already engraved on our hearts. All we have to do is decide that God's righteousness is superior to any standards we could manufacture on our own. By adapting to God's indwelling righteousness, we begin to hate evil and bless good.

Goodness

It's God's character to do good in every situation. The Bible's idea of goodness is when our actions are morally right and favorable for others. When we act out of completely unselfish motives and do things that benefit others, we are practicing goodness. Adapting our lives to the goodness of God is choosing to do the right thing regardless of the way we've been treated. (Look in 1 Peter 3:9.)

Truth

Truth is the solid ground you stand on no matter how hard the wind of trouble tries to blow you over. Truth stands when everything else falls. *Truth is.* (Read John 14:6.)

Someone committed to live by the truth in any situation says, "Let's do everything we can to work it out." I'm so glad that when it came to sending Jesus to pay our sin penalty that God operated in His truth. Being committed to truth gives us grace to hear, understand, and speak honestly to other people. We can listen and understand, because God has forgiven us so much.

Today our world says that truth is relative to each person and to each situation. We each decide on our own truth for our own lives.

If you agree with that, then it follows you must also believe that each of us lives in our own reality, created by our chosen truths. There can be no reality without truth. Truth is the foundation and parameter of all reality. As long as you continue to choose your own truth, you limit yourself only to that which you can discover and understand. Isn't it time for you to live beyond your own puny limitations? Isn't it time for you to accept the truth of God's Word? Isn't it time for you to start living in the limitless possibilities of God's truth for you?

2. ATTEND TO THE MINOR AREAS OF YOUR LIFE.

*"He who has clean hands and **a pure heart..."*** (Ps. 24:4, NIV).

Before the pilot takes off, he and his crew run down a checklist of major and minor things to make sure the plane is safe to fly. Minor things have a way of causing big disasters not only in planes, but in our lives. Many of the struggles we face are because we haven't developed in the small areas.

Convictions form our guiding philosophies. If you want to know why you made some of the decisions that now have you scratching your head, take a few minutes to clarify your convictions. Write out what you believe about:

- **THE MAKER** (you know, God)
- **METAPHYSICS** (things about faith, reason, the universe, eternity...you know, all the deep things)
- **MEANING** (the purpose for life, God's will)
- **MORALITY** (how you choose right and wrong)
- **MANKIND** (other people)
- **MAKING** (sexuality)

Intimacy with God
Developing intimacy with God helps you stay out of trouble in the areas of temptation you regularly face. **When you are in love with God, it's much easier to see past the temptation and into His eyes.** The more intimate we are with God, the less destructive we are in our relationships. He teaches us how to love others, as He loves us...unconditionally and unselfishly. He teaches us how to live lives of purity.

Personal Conviction
Convictions are based on commands and principles of Scripture. **A conviction is owned truth.** When you choose to own truth, you begin to form convictions. Truth is the solid ground you stand on when everything outside yourself crumbles. Convictions are what you stand on when everything inside you crumbles.

Your personal convictions are the greatest safeguards you have.

They are the basis on which God deals with you.

They are the means by which God matures you.

They are the means by which God directs you.

Your conviction about the Covenant principle of purity affects every decision you make. Stake your purity on the truth of God's Word, and every decision you make will be firm.

Healthy Responses

Jesus forgave. He was hanging on the cross, and just before He died, He said, *"Father, forgive them, for they do not know what they are doing"* (Luke 23:34, NIV).

Jesus wasn't being noble when He asked God to forgive the people who crucified Him. He was handling a difficult situation and difficult people with the unconditional love of God. That's the same way we need to handle the situations and people we find difficult.

"But we have the mind of Christ" (1 Cor. 2:16*b*, NASB). As we continue to adapt our lives to the indwelling Christ, His mind becomes ours, and we begin to respond to difficult people the way Jesus did.

One way God helps us develop healthy responses is to put us in a situation surrounded by people we can't stand, and then He says, "Love them."

Read through Philippians 2:5-11 and list the attitudes that make up the mind of Christ.

Verse	Attitude
5	
6	
7	
8	
9	
10	
11	

Corporate Identity

You belong to the body of Christ, so stay in church. You left home for school, but that doesn't mean you should leave the church. There are other members of Christ's body in your town who are incomplete without you. Find a church and get plugged in. If you can't find a church, you're not looking. **There is a dimension of God's power you can have only as a part of the corporate body called the church.**

3. ATTAIN MAJOR ACHIEVEMENTS.

The payoff of purity

"He shall receive a blessing from the Lord... This is the generation of those who seek Him, who seek Thy face" (Ps. 24:5, NASB).

We need a generation who is more committed to the issue of purity according to God's character than they are their own rights.

God says the person who seeks His face will receive a blessing from the Lord. Here are just a few of the ways God blesses those He likes to be around.

A friend of God

God counts you as a friend. The Creator of the universe and the Giver of Life calls you friend. He sees and knows everything, and there is nothing about you that is hidden from His eyes. God sees you as you are, yet loves you unconditionally. He could make us slaves, but because of His love, He calls us friends.

Security

When we have clean hands and a heart of purity, we have a security that can't be taken away. God's forgiveness and acceptance is a permanent part of our lives. His character can't be taken out of us.

Passion in worship

Psalm 24 is a worship psalm. The person of character is a true worshipper. The power of worship is determined by the heart of purity. The one who has molded his character to the character of Christ experiences greater passion in his worship. How pure is your worship?

Clean conscience

Intimacy with God will lead you to clean up your life. A heart of purity simplifies your thought life.

Blessed relationships

After you've developed a friendship with the Father of Life, how else do you think it will affect your relationships with others? Your relationships will be blessed. Since this session is about how to be a person people want to be with, you should be very interested in receiving this blessing.

Activity of God in your life

To those who are pursuing the character of Christ, He promises to protect us, provide for us, and promote us. God never stops His activity on our behalf.

4. ADVANCED THROUGH ACTIONS.

Establishing purity throughout our lives requires steady application. We must continually choose to offer ourselves to God in the details of our lives. In relationships, we won't sacrifice friendship with God for friendship with others. In relationships, all aspects of our actions will come from a heart of purity given to us by God.

> **"What's worse than having no Christian friends is having Christian friends who compromise their moral integrity."**

Between You and God

These questions are provided to help you pry open areas of your life to apply the truths of this session.

What characteristics do you have which would cause people to want to be with you?

Read John 1:35-39 and determine why you think these men wanted to be with Jesus.
(Being like Jesus will cause certain people to seek you.)

In what ways have you benefited from spending time with Jesus?

Name two or three people you really enjoy being with. Why?

How has another person benefited from being with you?

If you truly desire to be a person others want to be with, what changes would you need to make in your current lifestyle?

How can you reach "impure" people for Christ without being with them, and how can you be with them without becoming impure yourself?

Why does the person you are becoming influence the depth of your worship?

bulletproofing your life

Start with Christ, who lives in you.
Identify the seeds of self-destruction.
Manage your thought life.
Plan your personal convictions.
Live by design.
Exchange wrong decisions for right ones.

Bulletproofing Your Life

Top 10 favorite Christian choruses we sing, but never really expect to happen.

10.   "Jesus, Be Jesus in Me"

9.   "Let the Walls Fall Down"

8.   "Holiness Is What I Long For"

7.   "Give Us Clean Hands"

6.   "Take My Life, Lead Me, Lord"

5.   "I Wish We'd All Been Ready"

4.   "Friends Are Friends Forever"

3.   "You Are My All in All"

2.   "Lord, Prepare Me to Be a Sanctuary"

1.   "I Could Sing of Your Love Forever"

We sing these songs, and we really do want God to work His will in our lives. But when the melody fades and we're back at the everyday things of life, it's not so easy to choose God's will. One of the greatest challenges we face is to delete our personal agenda and allow God to have His complete way in us. The Scripture gives us a complete illustration of how this is done.

In Matthew 21:1-13, Jesus rode into Jerusalem on a donkey. Everyone welcomed Him with smiles as they called out His name. They thought He was going to be their political savior. They believed He would ride down the street and depose the tyrant king to make room for His kingdom. Instead of going to the palace, He went to the temple.

Jesus was full of surprises. When He went to the temple instead of the capitol, Jesus was doing exactly what He was sent to do. He came to build a kingdom, but first He had to establish purity in the temple.

This story is a metaphor for what Jesus does when we invite Him into our lives. When He comes to live in us, He begins to fulfill His purpose in us. He begins to build His kingdom in our lives. We still have an agenda we want our lives to follow. The specific expectations we have are probably not going to match up with His purpose. We are His temples, and we need to expect Jesus to clean us out.

Purifying the Temple

> When it comes to His temple, Jesus will purify it, then we are to protect it.

JESUS CONFRONTS SIN.

"And Jesus entered the temple and cast out all those who were buying and selling" (Matt. 21:12, NASB).

When Jesus got to the temple, the crowd was thick, and the noise level was high. The mixture of sights and smells reminded Jesus more of an open-air market than a place of worship. Money changers charged unfair rates to exchange currency for temple money. Merchants were selling inferior animals at inflated prices for quick and easy sacrifice.

Jesus walked into the temple and immediately saw what wasn't right. He wasn't afraid to tell the people just how far they had gotten off track. There was no way they could have missed the point of his words and actions. He confronted their sin.

There is no shortage of the sin targets in our lives. Jesus enters the heart temple and begins to expose the inside. If sin isn't being confronted in your life, you'd better check who's staying in the master bedroom of your heart.

Jesus confronts our personal sin, because He's after something greater in our lives.

We Want...	He Wants...
...our prayers answered	...our character changed
...to feel good	...to make us well
...to express our individuality	...our conformity to Christ
...God to speak to us about the future	...to deal with us about our present

---

GOD IS NOT A MACHINE. HE'S A KING.

In your own words, explain how we treat God like:

A slot machine

A rental car

A computer

Last summer I was in Houston meeting someone for lunch. Down the street from the restaurant a guy was standing on the corner begging. He asked me for money. I told him I was going to lunch and I'd be glad to bring him something back in about an hour. "An hour? I can't wait an hour!" Maybe it's me, but I said to him, "Hey, you're homeless. Do you have an appointment written down in a homeless day scheduler or something? You seriously don't have anywhere to go, do you?"

We're not that different. God wants to give us the food we need and we complain that we don't have any input about the menu. God provides us with the necessities of life, and we're mad because we don't get enough candy. He's after something greater than our momentary comfort. He knows that the only way to root out the sin in our lives is to confront it. His perspective is long-term...ours is short-term. His goal is to make us *clean,* not *comfortable.*

JESUS CHALLENGES THE STRUCTURE OF OUR LIVES.
"My house shall be called a house of prayer..." (Matt. 21:13*b*, NASB).

The temple market sold second-rate goods for premium prices (you know, like needless markup). The holy ground had become unholy. The temple structure had been built out of holy items so that a holy people could worship a holy God in holy ways. But the structure had been compromised to meet the agenda of greedy people.

Jesus challenged the greed of man-made authority. He called them what they were: thieves. He took a whip and literally threw out the merchants and money changers, turning over tables and breaking open cages. He completely challenged the structure of their lives. He knew what was being thrown out was nothing from heaven. Jesus saw the hell and drove it out.

When we sing, "Jesus, Be Jesus in Me," He will enter our lives like a king. He involves Himself in the details of our lives. This is the great irony. We want Him to be Jesus and fix everything, but we don't want Him to interrupt the structure of our lives.

There is no change without challenge. Jesus lives in us to change us into His character and image. This change will be challenging. But the good news is, if we allow it, the challenge brings eternal change in us.

Jesus looks at the structure of our lives and asks the hard questions about what we are making our lives into. Here are some blunt questions Jesus might be asking you. (Spend some extra time on these.)

Who are you trying to please?

If you're trying to please anyone other than Jesus, you're living below your purpose in life.

Which of your own needs are you trying to meet?

What insecurities are you holding on to? (for instance, failure, rejection, shame, etc.)

What feelings are running your life? (for example, resentment, unforgiveness, etc.)

What are the issues of purity competing for your heart? (for example, impure thoughts, focus on lesser things, etc.)

Every time we give place to one of these competitors, a part of the soul dies…it dulls our sensitivity to God.

What do you value the most? (comfort, success, sacrifice, lifestyle, etc.)

What are your expectations about God? (For some people, it is for God to be nice and leave them alone.)

What are you hiding from God?

What are you hiding from yourself?

What are you hiding from other people?

There are easier religions. The question is whether we are going to adapt our lives to the King of Kings. If we are, we have to examine ourselves to see if we reflect the ethics of the King (see page44).

HE CALLS FOR SURRENDER.

"For I say to you, from now on you shall not see Me until you say, 'BLESSED IS HE WHO COMES IN THE NAME OF THE LORD!'" (Matt. 23:39, NASB).

Surrender is not like a "tap-out" in the wrestling ring. It is abandonment. It's, "I've tried it, and I can't." It's releasing the control of your life and accepting what He has, regardless of the place, the plan, or the provision. It's more than raising the white flag and becoming a prisoner of war. Surrender goes so far as to cooperate with God to fulfill His plans, not yours. It makes every area of your heart open and accessible to His work.

Your relationship with Jesus is not romantic, so stop flirting with Him. Abandonment requires you to stop flirting and start following. Until you say, *"Blessed is He...,"* you will not see the fullness of what He has for you.

"Now to Him who is able to do exceedingly abundantly beyond all that we ask or think..." (Eph. 3:20, NASB).

The S.W.A.T. team of the city police department is the best of the best. They pay the price to stay in shape, they take the food supplements and put in the time at the gym. Their bodies are fit and ripped. But before they jump out of the van at a hostage situation, they strap on the Kevlar bulletproof vests to protect those bodies they have worked so hard for. We need to become Kevlar Christians. We need to bullet-proof our lives. It's the only way we can protect the surrender we have made.

> If you could become anything you wish, what would it be?

Protecting the Temple

The Christian life is not a playground—it's a battleground. There are no swings, slides, or sandboxes. The air is filled with bullets, bombs, and bayonets. The joyous sounds of celebration are most genuine when we have faced the conflict and won. We all like to win, but how do we increase our chances of winning? We bulletproof our lives.

We bulletproof our lives because the enemy is out to take our usefulness. The enemy is against the things of God that are in us. He hates everything about God, and that includes you. He will launch every possible attack and use every weapon imaginable to defeat us individually. First Peter 5:8 tells us to, *"Be alert!"*

The athlete prepares well in advance of the game. The pilot completely checks out the plane before takeoff. The bank balances the books before opening its doors. The band practices before the first note of the concert is played. And I take time to do "pre-game" before I get up to speak. The point is, the time taken to prepare for the fight is more important than the fight itself. Proper preparation involves some key steps. Here they are.

IDENTIFY THE STRUGGLES
"No temptation has overtaken you but such as is common to man" (1 Corinthians 10:13a, NASB).

We stay alert to danger by maintaining our fellowship with God. Through this intimate partnership, God helps us identify the danger zones in our lives. He gives us the wisdom to see our struggles, identify the causes, and avoid the situations. Without this help, we're doomed. Anyone who has fallen and gotten back up can fall back into the same sin again. No one is immune.

God limits the enemy in our life. The enemy is powerful, but not all-powerful. God allows the enemy no more power than we can withstand.

If you can't identify where you are being tempted, you'll be hit there again. If you can identify it, chances are you'll still get hit there, but at least you'll have the advantage of being able to prepare for the hit.

There are **two areas** to look for temptation to attack: **past failures** and **present fights.**

Past failures—Where have you failed before? You need to have a clear picture of the places, times, and situations where you have failed before. The more detail in the picture, the clearer the vision.

Present fights—Where are you struggling right now?

AHEAD TO THE PAST

Identify some of your past failures, so you can prepare for future attacks.

INVENTORY THE SPECIFIC SITUATION

"God is faithful, who will not allow you to be tempted beyond what you are able" (1 Cor. 10:13b, NASB).

You have to see a situation related to purity and holiness for what it really is. If you're going take wise action, you can't be fooled on any one part of the situation. If you are, sooner or later you'll act foolishly. Here are some questions that will help you take a quality inventory.

BACK TO THE PRESENT

Where are you struggling right now? Identify your struggles to help you prepare for the future.

Situation inventory

To make this most effective, be honest and write down the first thing that comes to your mind—your first unguarded response. Don't cheat; you'll only cheat yourself.

Inventory Your Purity
Why is this situation happening?

What were you thinking when it happened?

Where did it happen?

Place and time?

When did it happen? During a high time, or low time, or under emotional stress…?

Who did it happen with?

Who are the people who helped you into this temptation?

The enemy can attack and entice us into incredible rebellion. We must realize that we are as vulnerable as the next guy.

INITIATE THE SAFEGUARDS

"...but with the temptation will provide the way of escape also, that you may be able to endure it" (1 Cor. 10:13b, NASB).

You can stand against the schemes of the enemy. There is a power in you that is beyond you. When you focus that power on the temptation, the enemy can't have you. You are not a victim, but a victor.

Guard your heart. *"Above all else, guard your heart, for it is the wellspring of life"* (Prov. 4:23, NIV).

Change your oil every 3,000 miles. Scotchgard your Nubuc leather shoes. Brush your teeth. Wash your hands after visiting the toilet. These are all safeguards we do without even thinking. There are some key safeguards we have to initiate if we are to guard our hearts.

Read the Word. "My son, pay attention to what I say; listen closely to my words" (Prov. 4:20, NIV). The steady flow of Scripture over our hearts keeps them soft, pliable, and tuned to hear God's warnings and see the escape He provides. To fix a wrong, you must feed on the Word.

Operate in the strength of the Spirit. Our strength is limited. God's is not. Remember, the battle we fight is spiritual, not physical. You can't fight the spiritual battle without the strength of the Spirit. By keeping your life adapted to Him and living in obedience to His will, you strengthen yourself in the Spirit. (Check out the battle in 2 Corinthians 10:5.)

Have people in your life who can help you. A weight lifter has a spotter. The runner has a coach. The bookkeeper has an auditor. And the game has a referee. Without the spotter, the coach, the auditor, or the referee, there is no accountability. Our lives are much more important than a sport or a business, yet few of us ever make ourselves accountable to someone else. (Somebody needs you—Hebrews 10:25.)

Here's the kind of accountability you are looking for. Seek out people who encourage, support, and inspire you. Be open to people who know how to live and walk in the Spirit. Find people who are committed to growing and are consistent in their character. None of us can reach full potential without the help of other people.

Guard your eyes. *"Let your eyes look straight ahead, fix your gaze directly before you"* (Prov. 4:25, NIV).

Our world is full of attractive distractions as we seek to live a life of purity. Things to have, places to go, people to be with. The things we look at often distract us from focusing on what God is doing in our lives. It's not an easy safeguard, but it pays huge benefits. Don't lose sight of your first love…Jesus. Don't lose sight of what God is trying to do in your life. A lifestyle of purity is possible.

Guard your lips. *"He who guards his lips guards his life, but he who speaks rashly will come to ruin"* (Prov. 13:3, NIV).

Which words are more important? The words people say to you or the words you say to yourself? The words we say to ourselves are much more important than the words people say to us or about us. The words we say to ourselves about ourselves have the power to shape who we are.

Our words can make us open to an attack from the enemy. We can confess our way out of a temptation. Bulletproofing our lips trains us to verbalize what God's Word says about us. Bulletproofed lips refuse to speak the lies of the enemy.

Here are a few lies to avoid:
"I've always been this way…I can't help it."
"My parents were horrible parents. That's why I am the way I am."
"It's just too strong a temptation."

Remember, *"Death and life are in the power of the tongue…"* (Prov. 18:21a, NIV).

Guard your time. *"…making the most of every opportunity, because the days are evil"* (Eph. 5:16, NASB).

Put your life on a schedule. Unstructured time is dangerous. That's not to say you shouldn't have any free time. But too much free time can open the door for a great number of temptations. Bulletproof your time. Watch how you spend your leisure time. Never forget that your time is God's time, especially your free time.

Guard your friends. *"For you were once darkness, but now you are light in the Lord. Live as children of light (for the fruit of the light consists in all goodness, righteousness and truth) and find out what pleases the Lord. Have nothing to do with the fruitless deeds of darkness, but rather expose them"* (Eph. 5:8-11, NIV).

Be extremely careful about the people you allow closest to you. These are the people who will influence you the most. These are the people who will either lead you closer to God or lead you away.

> *"But I say to you, that everyone who looks on a woman to lust for her has committed adultery with her already in his heart"* (Matt. 5:28, NASB).
>
> **How does this verse apply to you?**

> *"Death and life are in the power of the tongue…"* (Prov. 19:21a, NIV).

If your friends are pulling you into temptation, have the courage to change your friends. Why do we value faulty friendship more than we do faithful friends? Why would you spend time with a bad person just because you've known them a long time? We should be committed to people because of who they are, not just because we feel drawn to them. *"Do not be misled: 'Bad company corrupts good character'"* (1 Cor. 15:33, NIV).

Closing Thought

The Kevlar Christian knows his limitations. The bulletproof life willingly chooses to identify struggles that regularly appear. Then he can inventory the situation, taking stock of the *why* and *who* of each situation and then initiate safeguards to head off the temptation in the future.

It might help to write these three affirmations down on a card and keep it handy. We all need to be reminded of these things regularly.

1. He owns the temple.
2. He is with me in the midst of temptation.
3. He provides the way of escape.

We are bulletproof because of what God has done for us.

Between You and God

These questions are provided to help you pry open areas of your life to apply the truths of this session.

How can you prevent "bulletproofing" from isolating you from the world you are trying to reach for Christ?

Recall times in your life when you felt vulnerable because you had not adequately guarded your (1) heart; (2) eyes; (3) lips; (4) time; (5) friends (see page 68). Write about them here.

Why is it so difficult to forgive ourselves when we fall, even after God has assured us of His forgiveness?

[ ] pride
[ ] lingering doubt
[ ] lack of faith
[ ] condemnation from others
[ ] fear of another failure
[ ] poor self-image
[ ] or _____

there's a right way
to handle wrong decisions

Start with Christ, who lives in you.

Identify the seeds of self-destruction.

Manage your thought life.

Plan your personal convictions.

Live by design.

Exchange wrong decisions for right ones.

There's a Right Way to Handle Wrong Decisions

When I was a kid, my mom would tell me, "Two wrongs don't make a right." She was correct. It takes three rights to make a left. There are right ways to handle things that go wrong. And there are right ways to handle wrong decisions.

We have all bought into ideas that seemed to be the right thing, only to find out later that we blew it. Below is a list of things that seemed like a good thing at the time...but really weren't. Enjoy the read.

Things that seemed like a good idea at the time:

- Street luging—what were they thinking?
- Staying out past curfew—until you realized that late and really late translated into more grounding and really, really grounded.
- Talking back to your parents—until you realized your mom had a great right hook.
- Ditching class—until City College, Circle K, and Dairy Queen refused your application.
- Getting drunk—until you regained consciousness riding a motorcycle home...and you don't own a motorcycle.
- Body piercing—until you rode your bike and your body whistled eight different notes.
- Running in a marathon—until you realized driving was quicker.
- Cheating—until you realized you were sitting next to the dumbest guy in class.
- Food dehydrator—until you tasted dried food.
- Smoking in the boys room—until you realized it was a song.
- Christmas colored plastic wrap—if the plastic wrap is green, how do you know when the food goes bad?
- Taking a pizza to the President—until you saw yourself on CNN.
- Playing catch with a javelin—I'd say it depends on who's doin' the catchin'.
- Having younger brothers to blame stuff on so you won't have to take the beating—until...oh, well, that's still a good idea.

SESSION 6
There's a Right Way
to Handle Wrong Decisions

We have a tendency to try to handle things in our own way in our own time and for our own purposes. When we do this, we will make a lot of wrong decisions. It can be tough to find the right way to handle wrong decisions.

We have to live with the consequences of our bad choices. Some of us just do a better of job of it than others. We try all kinds of ways to live with consequences. We deny them, ignore them, and blame other people. We try and hide from them with pills, needles, and bottles. We seek psychics, horoscopes, and hundred-dollar-an-hour shrinks to help us find ways to avoid the consequences. But the consequences are still there. They weren't meant to be avoided, they were meant to be faced. When you've made a bad choice, you can't avoid the consequences, but you can do something about them.

Here's how to handle wrong decisions the right way:

In Joshua chapter 9, Joshua made a covenant with the Gibeonites. The Hebrew people had left Egypt with God's blessing. In Canaan they began to take the land God had promised them. Every city they faced fell before them. Every army they approached was defeated, and fled. There seemed to be nothing that could stop them from taking the entire land. Nothing, that is, except a treaty for peace.

The Gibeonites sent a delegation to meet with Joshua to seek terms of peace. This group did everything they could to give the impression that they had traveled a long distance. Their clothes were worn out, their bread was hard and crusty, their wineskins were dried and torn, they were dirty, and looked as if they had traveled for weeks. Their appearance made their lies convincing.

They told Joshua that they were from a country far away. They had heard about the awesome things God was doing for the Hebrews and wanted to come and make peace. Joshua challenged their story, but after tasting their bread and taking a whiff of the delegates, he believed them.

That's when Joshua made his mistake. Joshua 9:14 (NASB) says that he made peace with them, but they *"did not ask for the counsel of the Lord."* Joshua acted before he sought God's counsel. It was only a couple of days before the truth was known. Joshua had been tricked by the Gibeonites, and everyone knew it. But what could they do? The deal was set. What was the right way to handle this problem? They couldn't kill them—they had sworn peace. They couldn't punish them, either.

In Joshua 10, Joshua showed us that leaders can live responsibly. He took specific steps to handle the consequences of his wrong decisions with honor and godliness. He understood that the consequences of his decisions affected the lives of every person he led. **The five steps Joshua took serve as a guide to help us deal with our negative consequences in the right way.**

Step One

STEP 1—RECOGNIZE THE MISTAKE. Joshua 9:14-15

Joshua knew his mistake. He did not seek God's counsel. Up until this time, he had done everything under the counsel of God. He had seen Moses operate this way, and he had learned to hear the counsel of God. He had consistently sought God's counsel and obeyed it.

Joshua could have said, "You guys lied to me. The deal's off." He could have chosen many other wrong ways of dealing with his wrong decision. Instead of wimping out, he dealt with it. He recognized his mistake and admitted it. Wow! What a concept for a leader to recognize his mistake, let alone admit it! Our country needs more leaders like Joshua who will recognize and admit their mistakes.

God is calling for a generation of young adults who will follow Joshua's example and willingly recognize and admit their mistakes. He wants you to stop playing the blame game every time you make a bad decision. He wants the denial to stop and the confession to start.

We now interrupt this outline for an important message about not getting a word from God.

THE DANGERS OF NOT GETTING A WORD FROM GOD

When we go into a situation without the permission of God, these things happen:

1. We are royally scammed. Joshua 9:4-6
We believe what we see rather than trust what God knows to be true. We put confidence in our judgement, forgetting that God's thoughts are higher than ours, and His ways far exceed our ability to understand. He is wisdom, and He offers what He knows to anyone who will simply ask.

> Someone else being bad doesn't give us the right to be bad in return.

2. We rely on our senses. Joshua 9:5,12-13.

Joshua made a promise to these people based on their dried wine-skins and their crusty bread. You can have what you think are the facts and the advice of highly qualified people. But in the end, all you have is how it looks. You can't be confident of God's blessing without a word from Him.

3. We resist the check of the spirit. Joshua 9:7

All of Joshua's men told him not to make the covenant. God provides us with a way to know when we are about to make a wrong decision. This is called a check in our spirit. Down deep where God lives in our hearts, something doesn't feel right. We may not be able to explain it, but we definitely know something about the situation just isn't right. Sometimes God uses another person to warn us, like Joshua's men did.

When you get this check in the spirit, it's time to seek God's counsel. Put off the decision and talk it over with God. He makes His infinite wisdom and knowledge available to you, if you will ask. *"But if any of you lacks wisdom, let him ask of God, who gives to all men generously and without reproach, and it will be given to him"* (Jas. 1:5, NASB).

4. It results in constant struggle. Joshua 9:18,21; 10:6-7

God never intended the Gibeonites to be slaves to the Hebrews. They became a burden to God's people. They provided cheap labor for the nation, but they had to be taken care of. Once they were enemies, but they became allies. They were a liability God never designed Joshua to have. They were extra baggage. When you get involved in a situation where you don't have God's permission, it will tap into the success of your life.

Students tell me they think they can date non-believers without any negative consequences. Their hope is to make them Christians after dating them for a while. What they fail to realize is the close emotional bonds that are formed by dating a non-believer are extra baggage God never intended them to have.

This must be remedied with Scripture. Getting a word from God is nothing mystical. You get a word from God by reading the Bible. Here are a couple of important tips on reading the Bible.

Read the Bible systematically. Don't take a single verse out of context. Instead, read the verses before and the verses after it to find out why it says what it says. Once you understand the context, take context into consideration. Make sure you have the big picture before you take action on what you think God is saying.

Here are some of the things we tell ourselves when we don't have a word from God. I call them, "Words When I'm Without a Word."

"I can turn this situation around."
"It's not my fault."
"It won't affect me."
"It feels right; it can't be wrong."
"I deserve it."
"I'm a victim."
"I wouldn't have done it if you hadn't...."
"I'll deal with that when I get there."

Read the Bible specifically. When you sit down, ask God to help you understand what you are reading. The Bible is God's Word. It comes from God's mind. That's the same mind that created the world and everything in it. Don't be so prideful as to think that you (a creature created by the Creator) can understand the depth of God's Word. Ask Him. He'll tell you what He means.

Read the Bible with sensitivity. Ask the Holy Spirit to apply the Scripture to your life. You may find yourself reading a verse, and it will literally pop off the page and into your heart. Suddenly you'll not only understand what God's Word means, you'll understand what it means for your life. When this happens to you, then you'll know that's the work of the Holy Spirit.

Here's a starting point if you are caught up in the consequences of your wrong decisions.

Recognize your needs.	Reaffirm the truth.	Rewrite the truth.
I'm miserable.	I have joy in Christ.	Galatians 5:22; Romans 14:17; Romans 15:13
I don't have any direction.	God is leading me step by step.	Isaiah 40:11; Jeremiah 20:11; Psalm 37:23; Ephesians 2:10
I feel powerless.	God indwells me and empowers me by His Spirit.	Romans 8:11; Ephesians 1:19; 1 Peter 4:1
I'm inconsistent.	God has given me faithfulness and discipline.	Romans 15:5; 2 Timothy 1:7; Galatians 5:22
I'm so negative.	I have hope in Christ.	Romans 15:13; Jeremiah 29:11; Psalm 62:5
I'm very impatient.	God has given me patience.	Galatians 5:22; Colossians 3:12-13; James 1:2-4
I worry all the time.	God provides for me. I can trust Him.	Matthew 6:31-34; John 14:27; 1 Peter 5:7
I am a weak person.	God has given me strength.	Ephesians 3:16, 20; Isaiah 40:29; 2 Corinthians 12:9

I am disobedient.	God is working in my life. He is making me obedient.	John 15:9-10; Romans 6;17; Ephesians 5:8-10
I'm so confused.	I have the mind of Christ and a sound mind.	2 Timothy 1:7; 1 Corinthians 12:16
God can't use me.	God has gifted me and will use me uniquely.	Romans 12:4-8; Ephesians 4:7, 11-13

We now return you to our original outline.

STEP 2—REMAIN IN COVENANT WITH GOD.

(Josh. 9:25)

I don't know many leaders who would have honored the covenant the way Joshua did. Joshua knew that to bail on the covenant would have said to everyone, "You can't trust me, my people, or my God." Instead of looking for ways to get out of the covenant, he kept the covenant and trusted God to make it right.

"The covenant must not be broken for the luxury of a wild emotion."

What would you have done if you were Joshua? Our tendency is to get angry and try to get out of the covenant. We want no part of anything that has the potential to bring us so much pain. Joshua's example should challenge us to stay in the covenant. Instead of seeking desperate measures to escape, recognize and admit your mistake, then remain in the situation, trusting God to work it out.

"Remain in the situation, trusting God to work it out."

> **Read Romans 8:28. How do you think this verse applies to this principle?**

STEP 3—RESPOND TO THE DEMANDS OF THE COVENANT. (Josh. 10:6-7)

Five kings led their armies against Gibeon. The Gibeonites were no match for these armies, and Joshua knew it. He had bound himself with a covenant to protect them. He could not refuse to help them and continue to honor God. **The demands of the covenant required a response.**

Joshua spoke with the Gibeonite leaders who told him to do whatever seemed right in his eyes. They were willing to fight their own war. They opened a door that would have allowed Joshua to walk away. It didn't matter to Joshua what it cost to fulfill his covenant to the Gibeonites. No demand was too great, no expense too high. There was no price on his honor.

We get into our wrong situations through not consulting God. The way to get out of them is doing the will of God in that situation by responding to the demands of that situation.

What mistake(s) have you made? Have you recognized it? Have you admitted it? Have you committed to remain in covenant with God? If so, that's great, but are you willing to respond to the demands that covenant will require? Every wrong decision we make has a right way to be solved. Climbing out God's way means you have to respond to the demands of your situation.

STEP 4—DELIVERANCE REQUIRES GOD'S HELP.
(Joshua 10:8-14)

God told Joshua not to fear the enemy but to march all night and meet them in battle. Think about it. What kind of general would march his troops all night and then ask them to fight without a rest? It didn't make sense, but Joshua obeyed. God's ways of handling our wrong decisions don't always make sense, but they work.

After marching all night, Joshua's men mounted a surprise attack. God used that attack to confuse the enemy. They began to retreat, and Joshua's men ran after them, slaying them as they ran. While they were running, God caused large hailstones to fall on them. More enemy soldiers died from hailstones than swords.

He caused the sun and moon to stand still in the middle of the day. God did one of the greatest miracles in the Old Testament to get Joshua out of a bad decision. The sun did not set for many hours. This allowed Joshua to completely destroy the enemy. Imagine what God could do if you waited for His help in your situation!

God performed one of the greatest miracles in the Old Testament to get Joshua out of a bad deal.

There is no situation so bad that God can't make it good if you will choose to handle your wrong decisions in the right way. The right way is God's will.

STEP 5—RECEIVE GOD'S DELIVERANCE.

(Joshua 10:24-41)
While the enemy troops were fleeing, the five kings hid themselves in a cave. Joshua found them and had the entrance blocked with boulders. When the battle was over, they brought the five kings to Joshua. He told his army commanders to not be afraid, but to put their feet on the necks of the kings and to slay them, because God would dominate their enemies for them.

Any wrong decision you make can be handled correctly by doing God's will. Submission to God's will does not put God's foot on your neck—it puts your foot on the neck of your problem. Handling your failures in your way magnifies the disaster. If thinking your way out of your problem were an option, wouldn't you have done it by now? You have nothing to lose trying it God's way.

Joshua led his troops on what could be called "Blood Bath—Tour of Domination" (and the T-shirts were really cool). God completely delivered all five cities into Joshua's hands. This is the ultimate deliverance from the enemy's attack. These five cities were cities God intended the Hebrews to inhabit. They would have been overthrown one at a time, but God worked through Joshua's obedience to make his wrong decision right. Instead of fighting five different battles, God accomplished it all in one.

There is no way you can figure out all the ways your wrong decisions can play out. There are too many variables. You can't make a wrong decision all good. That's God's job. Let Him do it. You do your job. Recognize your mistake and remain in your covenant with God. Don't let your pride lead you into making another wrong decision. Don't run from God—He won't chase you. He'll just wait for you to come back to Him. You're closer to Him right now than you will be if you run.

Once you willingly recognize your mistake and respond to the demands, then pay the price of staying in covenant with God. Be willing to get the help you need. Be willing to work at changing your habits, your friends, and your attitudes. It won't be cheap, but considering where you could end up, it's a bargain. Pay the price, and watch God do miracles for you.

Conclusion

This story is a metaphor for reestablishing purity.

God reestablished the **purity in His call** that He placed on Israel. His chosen people had repeatedly left Him to follow other gods. Through this experience, God demonstrates to His people that He is still their God, and they are still his people. God has not abandoned His purpose for your life. He still has a wonderful plan and future for you.

God reestablished the **purity of His covenant** with Joshua. The wrong decisions Joshua made could have derailed his leadership, but God reestablished Joshua as the one who would lead His people into the land of promise. God is fully committed to keeping every promise He has made to you.

God reestablished the **purity of His commission** to take the Promised Land. Even through their rebellion, God had led His people to take the land that He had promised would be theirs. In spite of what we've been through, our greatest days of blessing are ahead of us.

Take a moment and pray through these three things in your life:
• Ask God to remind you of His call and destiny for your life.
• Ask God to remind you that as you move back into covenant with Him, you move you back into His blessing.
• Ask God to empower you as you reestablish purity in your mind, heart, actions, and relationships.

The point of this session has been to show you that there is a right way to handle any wrong decision(s) you have made. God invites you to reestablish purity in any area of your life. *"Come to Me, all who are weary and heavy-laden, and I will give you rest. Take My yoke upon you, and learn from Me, for I am gentle and humble in heart; and YOU SHALL FIND REST FOR YOUR SOULS. For My yoke is easy, and My load is light"* (Matt. 11:28-30, NASB). Why not open yourself up to the possibilities of what God can do?

"He who loves purity of heart and whose speech is gracious, the king is his friend" (Prov. 22:1, NASB)

Between You and God

These questions are provided to help you pry open areas of your life to apply the truths of this session.

Think of a particular "bad decision" in your life and apply the five Joshua principles to it. (Step 1—Recognize the mistake, etc.; see page 75).

Based on the truths of these six sessions, write out your own personalized purity covenant with God.

Recall an incident in your life when you did the right thing even though it hurt you.

How should we relate to a person who has become sexually involved? Does God give a second chance? Can you think of a biblical example of this?

If you feel vulnerable in a particular area of your life (such as bad language, impure thoughts, impure activities, etc.), how would accountability to another person be of help?

Use the Temple Maintenance chart at right to assess your response to the CrossSeekers Covenant principle of *purity*.

Temple Maintenance

"...we are the temple of the living God... let us purify ourselves from everything that contaminates body and spirit..." (2 Cor. 6:16; 7:1).

AREA of CONCERN	Self-rating 0=low 10=high	Corrective Action Plan / Notes
1. **EXERCISE** aerobics, walking, active sports		
2. **REST - SLEEP** determine needed average hours and stick with it; get to bed earlier		
3. **NUTRITION** balanced diet, healthy food, limit certain foods; avoid obesity and bulimia		
4. **CONTAMINANTS** avoid drugs and tobacco products; develop a biblical stance on alcohol; avoid drunkenness		
5. **WEIGHT** reach and maintain proper weight		
6. **APPEARANCE** grooming, clothing, posture, cleanliness		
7. **SEXUAL ACTIVITY** living according to biblical standards; sex only within covenant marriage		
8. **SABBATH REST** taking one day in seven for rest, change of pace, worship, relaxation.		
9. **THOUGHT LIFE** "garbage in...garbage out" what you listen to, look at, think about; avoid pornographic materials		
10. **HEALTHY LIFE BALANCE** body, mind, soul, spirit, social contact. (Luke 2:52)		

leader's guide

holy
and acceptable

building a pure temple

leader's guide

The following general suggestions will help you succeed as a group leader for this CrossSeekers study. Then find suggestions for each of the six individual sessions.

Before the session:
• Read the Scripture passage for each session.
• Study the session before leading it.
• Pray for each group member by name.
• Set up the room.
• Make sure you can relate the Bible stories in each session.
• Look over the Leader's Guide for the corresponding session and be prepared.
• Arrive at least 15 minutes early.

Start the session:
• Start on time.
• Begin with prayer.
• Begin each session by sharing a brief thought based on the six simple beliefs that produce super-natural behavior found in the introduction. One of the simple beliefs goes with each of the sessions. Make sure to read the introduction.
• Remember, your attitude is contagious.

During the session:
• Encourage free exchange of ideas.
• Keep conversations aimed in the same direction.
• Don't allow one or two members to dominate (unless you only have one or two).
• Be sensitive to your group members. They may or may not want to share what they are thinking.
• If you have an idea that you think will work better with your group, use it.
• Remember, the idea is to help your group members learn something, whether or not you get through all the steps in the Leader's Guide.

Covenant Closing:
• Close the session on time.
• If you need to skip something, try not to skip the closing activity.
• Be sure to reaffirm the CrossSeekers Covenant principle of *purity* at the end of each session.
• Close in prayer.
• Clean up the room.
• Sit and think for at least five minutes about how the session went. This will help you be better prepared for next week's session.

Session One

A Moment of Clarity

Before the session:
• Study the session.
• Set up the room at least 15 minutes early.
• Have pencils ready.

Start the session:
• Start on time.
• Explain that the starting place for these studies is "Christ who lives in you."
• Open in prayer, asking God to help us understand the importance of Christ in us as the basis for our purity.
• Ask, *"How many of you have friends who say one thing and mean another?"* Invite group members to share some of their answers from the fill-in-the-blank section just under "He said. She said." section of session one.
• Ask, *"How do you think God defines purity?"*
• Ask if there is any student who wants to share which of the myths holds a position of power in their lives. Ask the group to bow their heads while you lead the group in the silent prayer printed at the end of the section on myths.
• Use the session materials (and anything else you can find) to tell the story behind Psalm 101. In this overview, be sure to take about five minutes to work through the "Powerful Results of Purity" found under principle one. Ask, *"When was a time you could have benefited from one of the powerful results of purity?"*
• Ask students to respond to this quote pulled from session one: **There are those things within us that we will not violate, and yet we seem to be tested at these points on a regular basis.**
• Ask students also to respond to this quote pulled from session one: **Purity isn't pulling weeds, it's growing roses.**

Covenant Closing:
- Review the CrossSeekers Covenant principle of *purity.*
- Bring enough salt packets for your entire group. Explain the significance of salt in the Bible. Salt enhances flavor and is a preservative. For our study, salt represents purity. Give each student a packet of salt. Ask them to tear it open. As they do, explain that salt is meant to preserve and protect. This exercise is symbolic of making a commitment to purity. Have each student pour the salt into their hand and put some on a finger. As they do, lead in a prayer that reaffirms the truths of this session.

Session Two

The Seeds of Self-destruction

Before the session:
- Bring a small package of sunflower seeds for the conclusion.
- Place a trash can in the middle of a circle of chairs.

Start the session:
- Start with prayer.
- Ask students to discuss their favorite scenes from the movies *Tommy Boy* or *Black Sheep.* Ask students to discuss the seeds of self-destruction found in the lives of Chris Farley and other stars.
- Take about 10 minutes and tell the story of Solomon from 1 Kings 11:1-14.
- Discuss with the students the list found in the section marked "Positive Deception."
- Ask students to respond to this quote pulled from session two: ***My good intentions will decrease the negative consequences of my actions.***
- Ask students to respond to this quote pulled from session two: ***You can trace every compromise back through these three things: thought, action, bondage.***
- Ask students to share from the pages of their "Diary of decay."

Covenant Closing:
- Review the CrossSeekers Covenant principle of *purity.*
- Pass around the bag of sunflower seeds, and ask each student to take about a dozen seeds. After everyone has their seeds, ask the students to place half the seeds in each hand. Then ask them to open their hands and look at the seeds in their left hand. Have them silently name the seeds with the seeds of destruction they have planted in their lives. After a few moments of silence, have them name the seeds in their right hand with the positive things they want God to plant in their lives. Lead them to pray silently while you pray aloud the prayer at the end of session two. After

the prayer, instruct the students to take the seeds from their right hands home and put them somewhere they will see them as a reminder for the next few days. Have them take the remaining seeds in their left hands and throw them in the trash can (placed earlier in the middle of the circle). This is symbolic of asking God to remove the seeds of destruction from their lives and the students making necessary choices in those areas..

Session Three

Session Three

Mental Floss

Before the session:
• Just before the session starts, call a local pizza delivery and order enough pizza for everyone in your group to have two slices. Time the delivery for about 25 minutes after starting the session.
• Prepare index cards with the following Scriptures on them: 1 Timothy 4:12; Romans 6:12-13; Romans 12:1-2; Proverbs 11:2; Proverbs 16:18; Romans 13:12-14.
• Ask a local dentist to donate samples of dental floss to use in the conclusion.

Start the Session:
Have the group arrange their chairs in a circle. Distribute paper and pencils to everyone. Ask everyone to write their names at the top of the paper, then pass it to the person on their left. When everyone has done this, instruct students to write (at the bottom of the page) something positive or something they admire about the person whose name is at the top of the paper. When finished, they are to fold the paper just so their words are covered, then everyone passes these papers to the left and repeats the process. This continues until everyone gets their paper. Ask everyone to read the comments silently. Ask if anyone was surprised by anything they read. Ask students to share some of the things written about them. Tell students to keep their papers as affirmations. Say, *"These are things the people in this room think about you. Image what God thinks about you!"*

When the pizza is delivered, put it on a chair or small table in the middle of the group. Tell the group they must tell you the secret of tonight's session before they can have any pizza. Whenever any one person tells the secret of this session, then everyone can have pizza. (The secret is: You can't floss with what you don't have. This means you have to hide God's Word in your heart before it can really do its work in your mind.) Let the students get frustrated before giving in and accepting something close to the right answer. While they are eating the pizza, tell the story of Jesus' temptation in the wilderness. Make sure to play up the "If you are..." phrases of Satan, and the "It is written..." statements of Jesus.

Distribute the prepared index cards. Ask students to read their Scripture, and have the rest of the students decide which temptation that verse applies to. Ask them to discuss how knowing these verses could help resist temptation. Lead them to reaffirm that the Word of God is living and active, not dead and dormant. Lead them to reaffirm the truth of 1 Corinthians 10:13: that God will always provide a way of escaping every temptation.

Covenant Closing:
• Review the CrossSeekers Covenant principle of *purity.*
• Give each student a sample box of dental floss and an index card. Have them write on the card the thoughts and emotions they struggle with. Allow a couple of minutes for reply. When they are finished, instruct the students to pair up. One student will hold the card while the other student takes a length of floss, wraps it around their index fingers, and uses the floss to cut the card. The student holding the card should hold the card edge-up, with their own fingers close together so, the card won't bend when the student with the floss begins to saw the card. The card should cut easily with the floss. This is symbolic of how God's Word gets into those hard-to-reach places and cleans out the bad stuff. After all the students have cut their cards, instruct them to roll up the two pieces of the card and wrap the dental floss around the two halves. This symbolizes the transforming power of God's Word. You were once bound by your thoughts and emotions: now you are bound by the Word of God. Close in prayer.

Session Four
How to Be a Person People Want to Be With

Before the Session:
• Study today's session.
• Get a rose for the closing activity.

Start the Session:
• Start with prayer.
• Ask, *"Who are the people you like to spend time with? Why?"*
• Discuss what David means when he talks about "clean hands."
• Discuss what David means when he talks about "a pure heart."
• Ask students to respond to this quote pulled from session three: ***The more you choose to bend your will to the perfect will of God, the more character of holiness comes out through you.***
• Ask students to respond to this quote pulled from session three: ***When you are in love with God, it's much easier to see past the temptation and into His eyes.***
• Lead students through a discussion of their basic beliefs found in the section "Personal Convictions."

Covenant Closing:
- Review the CrossSeekers Covenant principle of *purity.*
- Pass around a rose and ask everyone to take a petal. When the rose has made its rounds, say: Smell your rose petal. That petal still has the fragrance of the rose. When you are fully committed to the will of God, you are like a petal. You are the fragrance of God to those around you.
- Pray for the group to be the kind of people God wants to be with, and that everyone would carry His fragrance to others.

Session Five
Bulletproofing Your Life

Before the session:
Bring an inexpensive, small candle for everyone in your group. You'll also need matches or a lighter.

Start the session:
- Start with prayer.
- Ask students to share answers from the interaction box under the heading **"God is not a machine. He's a King."**
- Ask, "If you could become anything in life, what would it be?" "How do you think Ephesians 3:20 applies to this?"
- Spend some time asking students to respond to the questions under the section, "He challenges the structure of our lives."
- In the section titled "Initiate the Safeguards," spend some time reading the Scriptures listed there and discussing ways the students can apply these things to their lives.

Covenant Closing:
- Review the CrossSeekers Covenant principle of *purity.*
- Give everyone in your group a candle. Turn out the lights and light the candles. Explain that as the candle lights the darkness, Jesus confronts our sin. Just as the candle wax is soft and pliable, we must be soft and pliable as God challenges the structure of our lives The candle willingly burns to keep the flame alive. We, too, must surrender to keep His flame alive in our lives and to be bullet-proof.

Session Six

There's a Right Way to Handle Wrong Decisions

Before the session:
Get enough machine nuts for everyone to have one.

Start the session:
• Start with prayer.
• Tell the story of Joshua's wrong decision.
• Discuss with the students the "Consequences of not getting a word from God."
• Spend whatever time is necessary to read through the Scriptures that will help students recognize their thoughts, recognize the truth, and rewrite the truth. Be sure to help students apply the truth to their lives.
• Ask students to respond to this quote pulled from session 6: ***The covenant must not be broken for the luxury of a wild emotion.***
• Ask students to respond to this quote pulled from session 6: ***God's ways of handling our wrong decisions don't always make sense, but they work.***

Covenant Closing:
• Review the CrossSeekers Covenant principle of *purity*.
• Tell the following illustration: Every helicopter has one nut that connects the large rotor to the engine. It is called "the Jesus nut." If this nut fails while in flight, the helicopter will crash...thus, the name. When it comes to handling everything the right way, it boils down to handling it according to God's will.
• Ask the students to put the machine nut on a key chain as a reminder that their commitment to seeking, following, and doing God's will is the "Jesus nut" in their lives.

crossseekers resources

CrossSeekers Resources

CrossSeekers: Discipleship Covenant for a New Generation
by Henry Blackaby and Richard Blackaby

Discover the six CrossSeekers principles brought to life in a user-friendly, practical, story-telling format. This study sets the stage for an exploration of each CrossSeekers Covenant point. Biblical and contemporary examples of promises made, promises kept, and promises broken, along with consequences, bring the biblical truths home to today's college students.
• 9 sessions • Interactive in format • Leader's helps included • $8.95
• ISBN 0-7673-9084-9

CrossSeekers: Transparent Living, Living a Life of Integrity
by Rod Handley

Integrity. Everyone talks about it. God *delights* in it. We *demand* it. But what exactly *is* integrity, and is it important? If you want to be a person of integrity, to live the kind of life Christ modeled— to speak the truth in love, to stand firm in your convictions, to be honest and trustworthy, then *Transparent Living, Living a Life of Integrity* is for you! This study supports the CrossSeekers Covenant principle *integrity.*
• 6 sessions • Leader's guide included • $6.95
• ISBN 0-7673-9296-5

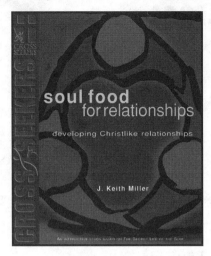

CrossSeekers: Soul Food for Relationships, Developing Christlike Relationships
by J. Keith Miller

Our relationships with other people are key to happiness and success in life. Too often, though, these relationships become stressful and unhealthy. How can we keep them Christlike? J. Keith Miller examines the false personality we create that leaves us feeling lonely, fearful, doubtful. Confronting this constructed personality and dismantling the self-created aspects lead us to authentic living and Christlike relationships. This study supports the CrossSeekers Covenant principle *Christlike relationships.*
• 6 sessions • Leader's guide included • $6.95
• ISBN 0-7673-9426-7

CrossSeekers: Spiritual Intimacy, Drawing Closer to God
by Glen Martin and Dian Ginter

Spiritual Intimacy will intensify the desire of your heart to know God more intimately, help you realize where you are in the process of drawing closer to God, and show you how to move ahead by knowing God on six successive levels. This study supports the CrossSeekers covenant point *spiritual growth.*
• 6 sessions • Interactive in format • Leader's guide included • $6.95
• ISBN 0-7673-9427-5

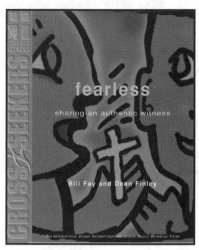

CrossSeekers: Fearless, Sharing an Authentic Witness
by William Fay and Dean Finley

Fearless, Sharing an Authentic Witness will equip collegians for sharing their faith with others. Sessions address concepts such as our lives as a living witness (using the CrossSeekers Covenant points for discussion), how Jesus shared with persons He met, learning where God is at work in another person's life, a threat-free and effective method for presenting the gospel, and addressing difficult questions/situations. Based on *Share Jesus Without Fear,* this study supports the CrossSeekers Covenant principle *witness.*
• 6 sessions • Interactive in format • Leader's guide included • $6.95
• Available 7/99 • ISBN 0-7673-9865-3

CrossSeekers: Gifted! Serving in Christ's Name

Gifted! Serving in Christ's Name examines spiritual gifts given by the Holy Spirit to each believer and leads collegians to discover their gifts and how to use them in service for Christ. A spiritual gifts inventory is included to enable collegians to determine their gifts. Collegians using their gifts in various service will be profiled, and opportunities for service will be highlighted. Collegians will be challenged to find a place of service utilizing their gifts. This study supports the CrossSeekers Covenant principle *service.*
• 6 sessions • Interactive in format • Leader's guide included • $6.95
• Available 7/99 • ISBN 0-7673-9853-X

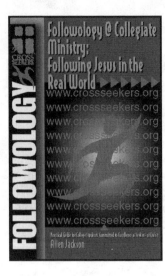

Followology @ Collegiate Ministry: Following Jesus in the Real World
by Allen Jackson

How well do you follow as a Christian? *Followology* is designed for the college student or young adult who is serious about following Jesus. Through an informal, interactive study, collegians will learn to follow the One who knows the way, because He *is* the Way!
• 8 sessions • Interactive in format • Leader's helps included • $9.95
• ISBN 0-7673-9083-0

Transitions: Preparing for College
compiled by Art Herron

For high school juniors and seniors *and their parents.* Practical help for the transition from high school to college—the admissions process, financial aid, loans and scholarships, lifestyle changes, spiritual development, and more!
• 6 sessions • Leader's helps included • $7.95
• ISBN 0-7673-9082-2

For more information, visit our Web site: www.crossseekers.org.